Prärieblomman:

The Prairie Blossoms for an

Immigrant's Daughter

Prärieblomman:

The Prairie Blossoms for an Immigrant's Daughter

Linda K. Hubalek

Butterfield Books

Aurora, Colorado / Lindsborg, Kansas

Prärieblomman: The Prairie Blossoms for an Immigrant's Daughter
1993 by Linda K. Hubalek

Fourth Printing 1996
Printed in the United States of America,

Cover design: Diane Steiner
Consulting Editor: Howard Inglish
Cover photo: Alma Eleanor Swenson Runneberg
Photos and maps courtesy of:
    Bethany College, Pages 62, 79, 80, 94, 97.
    Verna Berry, Pages 35, 70, 93.
    Alice Bohn, Cover page, xii.
    Kansas State Historical Society, Page 127.
    Rozella Schaeffer, Pages viii, 2, 40, 44, 48, 54, 81, 84, 92, 98,
                  104, 111, 116, 118.
    Smoky Valley Genealogical Society and Library, Pages 109,
                  121, 122, 124, 126.

Publisher's Cataloging in Publication
(Prepared by Quality Books Inc.)
Hubalek, Linda K.
    Prärieblomman: the prairie blossoms for an immigrant's daughter
/ Linda K. Hubalek. --1st ed.
    p. cm.
    Includes bibliographical references
    Pre-assigned LCCN 93-78406.
    ISBN 1-882420-01-2.
1. Swedish Americans--Kansas--Fiction. I. Title.
PS3558.U22P73 1993   813.54
                  QBI93-761

For information about Hubalek's books, see the list on page 128, or write to Book Kansas!/Butterfield Books, PO Box 407, Lindsborg, KS 67456.

To the grandmothers, mothers
and daughters who lived on this farm.

Everyone of us turned the doorknob on the parlor door, climbed
the steep staircase, planted the same garden and loved the land.

Books by Linda K. Hubalek

Butter in the Well
Prärieblomman
Egg Gravy
Looking Back
Trail of Thread
Thimble of Soil
Stitch of Courage

Acknowledgments

A very special thanks to Alice Runneberg Bohn, the daughter of Alma Swenson Runneberg, *Prärieblomman*'s main character, who wrote me a little note saying how much she enjoyed reading about her grandmother in *Butter in the Well*. It was her contact and interest that sparked the idea to write a sequel to carry on the story of the homestead's first family through the next generation.

I thank the same group of people that helped with *Butter in the Well*, as they pitched in again to research its sequel, *Prärieblomman*. Without the help and support of the Swenson, Runneberg, Olson and Peterson families, I would not have continued this project. Interviews with Liberty Township neighbors and people from the area towns have given me the information to re-create life during the 1890s. Their memories are what makes this farm area so special to its inhabitants, and the readers of this book.

I wish to express special gratitude to my family for their support in my latest adventure. I'm glad I grew up on the farm in Liberty township.

Tack så mycket.

Linda Katherine Johnson Hubalek

Table of Contents

Peter and Kajsa Runeberg

Prärieblomman

Foreword

My first book, *Butter in the Well,* was written as a fictional diary, dated 1868 to 1888, based on the real life facts of Maja Kajsa Swenson Runeberg, who homesteaded my family's farm in Saline County, Kansas, in 1868. Through research and interviews I found the detailed past of this Swedish family trying to make a home on the native prairie.

Readers of the book contacted me wanting to hear the rest of the story about the family in *Butter in the Well.* So I wrote this sequel, *Prärieblomman: The Prairie Blossoms for an Immigrant's Daughter,* using Alma Eleanor Swenson, the third child of the family, as the main character. The book starts in 1889 when Alma turns sixteen, and ends in 1900 when she marries at age twenty-seven and leaves Kansas.

Born in 1873, Alma grew up during the first hard years in America as her Swedish immigrant family carved a farm out of the prairie grassland. She knew first-hand the hardships, trauma and work it took to become a thriving homestead, and she looked forward to better years ahead as she matured into a young woman.

As a young adult with one foot planted in the old Swedish customs, she reached out to grasp the new American age. Although not forgetting her humble past, she embraced the changes and prosperity of the growing community and the mighty nation adopted by her parents. New inventions, increased modes of transportation and knowledge of the world through newspapers and magazines expanded the horizon of Alma's prairie.

I compare Alma's growing up to the word "prärieblomman," the Swedish name for prairie flower. Through her thoughts in her diary, we watch this immigrant's daughter blossom into a new life of her own.

In the early 1900s there were a series of annual books written in Swedish called *Prärieblomman*, published by the Lutheran Augustana Book Concern of Rock Island, Illinois. Each year they published a book of short stories featuring people, places and topics that were of interest to the Swedish-American communities that had settled around the United States. Bethany College and the Smoky Valley region of Kansas were frequent topics because of their Swedish ties. Although only 2,500 copies were printed each year, these books were also sent to Sweden to let the 'mother country' know the progress her native people were accomplishing in their new country.

I have in my possession a copy of *Prärieblomman: Kalender för 1903*. Ninety years later this Swedish book emerges in a new American form to remind us of our heritage. As *Prärieblomman* linked Swedish-Americans together in the 1900s, it is my hope that this book will connect today's generation with the past. By reading Alma's story, you absorb our nation's history and realize that the advancements our forefathers made yesterday affect our times and lives today.

To help you understand the people and area written about in *Prärieblomman*, I have included, in the back of the book, a family chart listing the main characters, a Swedish glossary and maps of the townships and towns mentioned. Please note there were no maps of the townships made between 1884 (featured in *Butter in the Well*) and the 1903 township maps in this book. You may not be able to find some families on the maps because they moved in and out of the township between this time, or they were renters instead of landowners.

Prologue

January 27, 1889

To Alma,

For your sixteenth birthday, I am giving you a blank book of pages. This may seem odd to you, but I want you to write down the normal, and unusual events that happen in your life. You don't have to write everyday. Just scattered tidbits of thought, misgivings and joy will record the growth in yourself and the happenings in the world around you.

Years later this book will bring back smiles and tears to help you recall favorite places you never meant to forget, cherish lives lost, and to see how yesterday's events become tomorrow's history. Someday you may want to show your children the changes you saw while growing up on this farm in Kansas.

Keep this book with you always. Your written memories will sustain you when you have moved on to a prairie of your own someday.

With love, Mamma

The Setting

Snow blankets the homestead on this quiet Sunday afternoon in 1889. Silent white-iced furrows in the fields of the 159 acres wait for spring planting. The height of bare-branched trees show the farm to be about twenty years old. You can tell that the farmer is prospering because there are several outbuildings, and the wooden two-story house has been added onto a time or two.

The dirt road running by the farm was just a trail not too many years back. Life and growth have progressed for the family, but there are still patches of native grass beside the homestead to remind them of their start on the prairie.

Peering into the parlor window facing south, you get a glimpse of petite Alma Swenson, an optimistic young woman with typical Swedish blonde features, innocently pondering her life as she turns sixteen.

Alma Eleanor Swenson

1889

The Birthday Present

January 27

Sunday dinner dishes are done, little sisters are napping, and I have a few moments to myself. As I turned the white porcelain door knob and slipped into the cool, closed-off parlor, I pondered about the book of blank pages Mamma gave me today for my birthday. On the first page, she wrote a note, encouraging me to write.

Mamma has kept a diary ever since she moved to Kansas in 1868. I've never read it myself, since it is personal, but sometimes Mamma reads bits to us. A diary entry may make her smile or bring tears to her eyes.

Her journal tells the trials and errors as she and Papa built their homestead on the virgin prairie twenty years ago. When they arrived as Swedish immigrants to this land by the creek, the blue stem grass was as high as a man's head on horseback. With their bare hands and a few primitive tools they cleared the land, dug a well and fashioned a sod dugout home. Clashes with Mother Nature, Indians and animals as they struggled to coax crops out of the broken sod almost took their toll on Mamma's spirit, but she had a family to feed and protect. Favorite entries tell when her children were born and the joy of uniting with families when my grandparents left Sweden and moved to America.

The dugout was replaced by a sandstone one-room house in 1870. The house has been built on to three times with wooden additions when we could afford to buy lumber. The barn and granary were originally makeshift buildings for temporary storage of the crops and animals. As of yet they have not been replaced. A sod and straw-roofed open shed shelters the animals when they are out in the elements and the chicken house guards the fowl flock at night. Most of the acres of prairie have been tamed into fields for crops except for the hay meadows along the creek.

The Farm

Us older children are almost grown now. Christina is twenty-two and getting married next month. Willie turned nineteen the fourth of this month and Alfred is fifteen. Carrie, who was born after Papa was killed, is twelve. When we needed help on the farm, Peter Runeberg came into our lives as a hired hand, and five years later he and Mamma were married. Our half-sisters, Julia, born four years ago and Mabel, last March, have livened up and further crowded our household.

Peering out the window at the drab sleeping field to the south, I ponder over Mamma's note. Maybe someday I will cherish my thoughts and reflections, the everyday events that have taken place on our farm. I wonder, since I finished my country schooling last year . . . what will my future bring? Will I marry soon and start a family or spend my life here on my Mother's farm, tending to the everyday tasks that must be done to sustain life? With ten of us in the house, counting the Star School teacher that sometimes stays with us, there is always plenty to do.

January 28

It's hard to think of anything exciting to write in my diary since most of my waking hours are spent at home, doing everyday chores repeated every week, slightly changing the routine with the season or weather.

Even though it's freezing outside today, I was up to my elbows in hot sudsy water this morning scrubbing dirty shirt collars and skirt hems on the washboard. Steam rising from the near boiling water almost prevented me from seeing my work, but kept me warm at the same time. Unless there's a blizzard or it's raining on Mondays, it's a weekly job that has to be done outside because we have to heat the large iron kettle of water over an open fire. After the wash had freeze-dried on the clothes line, we brought the stiff-as-a-board clothing into the house. Slowly the stacked shirts become a pile of clean damp clothes again.

Tomorrow morning we'll go through the pile to mend any new holes or tears. The next step in the process is to press the wrinkles out of our laundry. I've learned to tell if the flat iron heated on the top of the stove is hot enough, by quickly touching my wet finger to the bottom to see if it sizzles the right sound. We press everything from shirts and petticoats to bed sheets, so it's an all day job.

February 6

The kitchen table legs thumped the floor in rhythm this morning as Mamma kneaded and pounded the bread dough for the multitude of mouths we feed every meal. This is a ritual that has happened probably every Wednesday and Saturday of Mamma's entire adult life.

Several hours a day are spent preparing the three meals for our large family (not mentioning washing the all dishes). We use several half-gallon jars of canned meat, vegetables and fruit each day. There's a routine: whenever someone goes down to the cellar for food, they take down washed empty jars. Slowly as summer approaches, the shelves that were loaded with colorful jars of food last fall, are refilled with empty jars ready to start the process over again.

Another endless job is trying to keep the floor clean. Although we sweep the dirt and barnyard manure out the back door every morning, one person can walk in and it looks like you never swept.

February 15

The winter evening light was fading fast as I trimmed the wick and polished the chimney on our dining room table lamp. As the glow lit the room, we gathered around the light to work on various projects.

Sewing Christina's wedding dress of gray wool with black velvet trim, and enough clothes and linen for their first years of marriage have kept us girls busy the last few months. Mamma said we'll start making quilts and household linens for my trousseau next.

As one of us finished reading the four-page newspaper we'd pass it on to the next person around the table. Winter can cut us off from the world, so newspapers link us to what is happening outside the perimeter of our farm. I find it fascinating that I can be sitting on a homestead on the Kansas prairie and read about events happening elsewhere. But sometimes I really do feel isolated when we can't get into Bridgeport for the mail and paper.

Today's *Assaria Argus* newspaper reports that it is thought that Jack the Ripper has been found at Dundee, Scotland. He is charged with murdering his wife in the same barbarous fashion as the others. He has made a confession and is believed to be insane.

Closer to home, the opening of the Indian Territory for settlement in the near future is attracting much attention throughout the country. Oklahoma, as the new territory is to be called, is said to be one of the finest sections of the West. Development will not take place until after the Indian titles have been resolved and the President issues his proclamation inviting settlement.

Reading the advertisements in the square boxes lining the margins of the paper can be an education in itself or provide the merchandise you need. I saw an ad for an illustrated catalogue for Root's Northern Grown Seeds, saying most packets are 3 cents each. We save most of our seed from the year before to plant the garden the next season, but I love to look at catalogues and dream of spring when the garden is full of green life, instead of covered with snow.

February 20

Sister Christina's wedding day. She and Swan Nelson were married in Salina by Reverend Floren of the Swedish Lutheran Church. Life will be so different for her, living in the big town of Salina, instead of the country. We won't get to see her as often, since she is now 16 miles away. Swan has a good job with Holmquist Implement, so she will have an easy life compared to women on the farm. What a contrast their big wooden-frame house is compared to the dugout she first lived in when Mamma and Papa moved to the prairie. It was strange to have her pack her things this morning in the room we've always shared. Julia will be moving upstairs to Christina's bed this spring, so Carrie and I won't be alone for long.

February 23

Shades of gray covered the heavens down to the horizon today. Just a light streak of silver between the sky and the earth, with no sun to warm the white ground. The silence was broken by the train lumbering through the section, then screeching to an unplanned halt. Ducking out of the chicken house, I could see the engineer jumping off his platform and walking around to the front of the massive engine. Peter and Willie, who were in the corral feeding cattle, walked across the plowed field to the train. One of our yearling calves had got out of the pen and wandered onto the track. In today's weather, the engineer didn't see the animal in time to stop. There wasn't enough of the poor thing to butcher for meat. At least the engineer told Peter he will be reimbursed by the railroad for the loss of the calf.

February 26

Overnight, our bare land that was almost ready to give into spring was shut down by a snow storm. It was like God had sifted snow through a flour sifter onto the prairie. Willie had talked about going to Assaria to the literary meeting tonight but weather has a way of changing our plans. I would have liked to have gone too, but I'm not sure Mamma would have let me go since I'm getting over a cold. Seems like everyone has had one lately. I'll read about the program in Friday's newspaper. I hope we can get to next month's meeting since it will be the last of the season.

March 4

Winter squeezes us all into the tight quarters of the house. At times I wish there were less of us, but I wouldn't want to get rid of anyone in our family! As the weather warms, we gratefully ease out into the sunshine to add new jobs to our list of chores to do. My brothers do most of the outside chores during the winter, but as longer days and spring work keeps them out past the perimeter of the farmyard, Carrie and I take over the evening milking and feeding of the cows.

Warm breezes of March were in the air today. Spikes of bright green wheat are poking their blades through the last patches of snow. With all the winter moisture we've had, the crop should be good.

Because Star School is barely a quarter of a mile away, I could hear the children today as they ran out to explode their energy at recess. Chicken-pox has curtailed the attendance of many children these last few weeks, but they have recovered and returned, ready to see their friends and renew their bond with the books.

Carrie says they have been studying about our United States leaders since Benjamin Harrison was to have been sworn in today as our 23rd president. I like to hear what the classes have been studying because I still miss school.

March 16

I inwardly sighed at the sound of the hymnals being shut in union after we sang the last song this evening. Tonight was our last night of singing school for the season. Roy Lamkin was a good teacher and kept us spellbound with his guidance. Even though Wheeler School, where it was held, is three miles away, we were able to make it almost every time. I love to sing.

I found out tonight Ida and Nellie Wheeler get to spend the summer at the Salina Normal University. I wish I could go too, but Mamma thinks I've had enough schooling.

The next step in life is marriage, but I'm too shy to flirt and talk to the boys like some of the girls my age. Minnie Granquist, one of my best friends in the neighborhood, is so at ease with talking to the opposite sex. At eighteen, she is a dark-haired beauty that turns the heads of most of the Liberty Township boys.

March 23

Tonight we went to the South Saline County Educational Association meeting at Bridgeport. Tonight's topics were How to Prevent Whispering, Geography and Course of Study. The Assaria and Bridgeport choirs and a male quartette provided the musical entertainment.

I talked to several friends during refreshments to find out what's going on in the neighborhood. L. S. Lamkin, our neighbor on the southwest quarter of our section has traded his farm for property in Lindsborg. Pete Olson's children have been sick with lung fever, but they are over the worst of it. Eva Fore has shingles. Mr. Lapsley, our black neighbor, must be under the weather too because he wasn't at the meeting tonight. He never misses a community gathering!

The wife of Blacksmith Morrison at Bridgeport had a twelve-pound baby girl Thursday morning. Mamma and the other women have been making comments all night about the pain of having that big a baby.

The men's side of the room talked about the joint debate between Assaria and Mentor that took place Tuesday night. The question debated was if the direct tax bill should be signed by the President.

March 27

Little sister Mabel's first birthday. I made a sponge cake and Carrie whipped cream for topping for the celebration. We set the cake in front of her to see the reaction. Using both hands she dove into the carefully frosted creation, squeezing the topping between her chubby baby fingers. Grabbing a handful of cake out of the center, Mabel tried to stuff it into her mouth, but most of it fell into her lap and on the floor. When Mabel wiped her hands on the front of her dress I understood why Mamma said "no!" to chocolate birthday cake.

Christina rode the Union Pacific train from Salina to Bridgeport, then followed the Missouri Pacific tracks across the river bridge and walked the two miles home for a surprise visit. It was the first she had been home since her marriage, and we had so much to talk about. As we toured the farm to show her the new colt in the barn and budding trees in the orchard, I tried to quiz her about happenings in Salina, but Christina longed for news of Liberty Township instead. Mabel and Julia constantly clung to the folds of Christina's long skirt.

Even though Mamma had explained over and over why their big sister left last month, they thought she had vanished forever.

March 28

Heavens crashed their cymbals and pulverized the township with rods of lightning last night. Peter walked the creek meadows this morning to check the cattle which had weathered the storm. Due to their height, the trees along the creek sometimes attract the bolts. The tallest cottonwood had a searing slash from the top of the tree to its sprawling roots, with wood splinters scattered twenty feet around the base. Situated on higher ground, our neighbors Mr. Swanson lost a calf to the lightning and Mr. Wheeler a horse.

The wooden floor creaked last night in the late hours as Mamma paced in the dining room during the storm. Lightning altered her life a dozen years ago and she still cringes when lightning strikes nearby. Even though time has clouded our young memories, we all remember the bolt that killed Papa when he was walking home in a storm.

March 30

The Bridgeport baseball club was practicing today when we were in town to trade for groceries. The team will soon start the season and play Roxbury, Gypsum City, Assaria, Lindsborg and Salina. Peter couldn't resist pulling up the reins on the horses as we came upon the field, and in that second all of us spilled out of the wagon to watch the game for a while. Shouts of encouragement mixed with the whistle of the first robins in the trees above the river bank. The steady thumping of the flour mill water wheel echoed above the muffled roar of the water cascading over the dam. Yellow dandelions popping up on the tender grass field were smeared on pant legs as the boys slid into the bases. Spring is here.

April 21

Gorgeous weather outside, but a little stuffy inside our Assaria Swedish Lutheran Church for the young people standing up for confirmation today. Half of the class were young people from our area: cousin Axel Johnson, Perry Lundahl, Swen Olson, Emma Almquist, Maria Johnson and Elsa Rundal. I sympathized with them as they stood in front of the congregation, sweating as they recited the passages memorized from the catechism book and Bible. I found myself murmuring the words myself since I went through it last year. When the relieved class lined up outside in the cool breeze after the service, we congratulated them on finishing their Lutheran studies.

April 26

The *Assaria Argus* reported that part of the Indian Territory of Oklahoma opened up to homesteaders on the 22nd. Willie talked of nothing else at the dinner table today. He'll probably always be a farmer, but he wants to do some traveling and I think Willie wished he could have been there to see history happen.

Because the new land to be opened was in the middle of the territory, the boomers were allowed to cross the line at Arkansas City, Kansas, and cut across the fifty-eight mile Cherokee Outlet four days before the race. Trains also ran to the opening land, but most traveled by horse or wagon. Due to the flood stage of the Salt Fork River, the army laid flooring down on a railroad bridge so the wagons could cross the river to get in position on the starting line on time. At high noon last Monday, 50,000 people rushed in by fast horses, railroad trains, stages and over 4,000 assorted wagons into the coveted territory. About 10,000 people got possession of all the desirable land, the newspaper reported. Many dreams were crushed when broken equipment, slow or injured animals hindered the unfortunate from staking claims. Overnight the tent cities of Norman, Guthrie, Oklahoma City, Kingfisher and Edmond sprang up on the open prairie.

April 30

Being a little late made it hard to crowd the nine of us in an already crowded church tonight. The special program we rode into town for observed the centennial of President Washington's inauguration. Professor Nelander of Bethany first spoke in English about his recent trip to Paris, and then he spoke in Swedish about Washington's inauguration and the first century of America. Patriotic choir and band numbers rounded out the program. Julia and Mabel fell asleep on the way home as the wagon rumbled along in the dark, the horses following the road back to their barn.

May 5

The Robinsons and Mr. Lapsley stopped on their way home from Wheeler School this afternoon to visit. Pastor Lucas, the Mentor

Methodist circuit preacher, gives services there at 3 o'clock on certain Sundays. Mamma insisted they stay for supper, so Carrie ran out to the chicken house to see if there were any more eggs laid since this morning's gathering to stretch our meal. Mamma wrapped the last of the fried chicken and biscuits in a cloth-lined basket to send home with Mr. Lapsley for his meal tomorrow. I stuck in a small branch from our blooming lilac bush to put a smile on his face. Knowing him, there will be something special tucked inside that basket when he brings it back.

May 10

Read in today's newspaper that Sterling, Kansas, had a tornado last Monday. The cyclone destroyed twelve barns, five houses, one school and one church.

This news, plus the fact that we were up and down the cellar steps several times this morning, made Mamma reminisce to Julia and Mabel about the time we took shelter in the cellar for the tornado that came through our farm in '76. Willie remembers the debris scattered around the neighborhood and picking cherries off the tree that had blown over in our orchard.

We hauled the oleander out of its winter spot in the cellar stairwell and set it on the porch to bloom until cold weather sets in again. The spindly geraniums that stretched for light downstairs were cut back and planted in the front flower beds today. In a few weeks they will fill out with new fuzzy green leaves and red flower buds.

May 16

I was leaning over the opening of the well with my back to the road and just about jumped out of my skin when I heard someone clear his throat behind me. I'm used to hearing horses and buggies, so I didn't hear the man approach. First time we ever had a bicycle on the farm, and its rider was an implement salesman. The gentleman was riding the bicycle around the county calling on the farmers. He said he's covering an average of 60 miles a day! I think he's fibbing a bit, knowing he's probably carrying that bicycle through some mud holes on our Liberty Township roads. He is certainly getting his exercise.

May 17

Guinea egg-size hail pelted our fields as a torrent of water gushed from the sky last night. In the early dawn light, we peered down the alley to the meadow where we could see the creek water overflowing from its banks, flooding all the bottom fields in its path. All legs scurried to move everything possible out of the outbuildings so things wouldn't be spoiled in the flood water or float away. Piled sacks of feed, buckets of tools and harnesses were thrown onto the wagons and moved east of the house. Alfred and I tied the horses and milk cows to the front yard fence while Carrie called the cats out of the barn. The flood water surrounded the farm, but never got as high as the buildings before it crept back in its place.

May 21

We were cut off from the world until the floodwater receded today. Alfred and Willie walked the tracks to Bridgeport to get the week's worth of mail. All of Bridgeport flooded because the river water was held in by the railroad grade that curves around the north and west sides of town. People were still shoveling stinking slime out of their houses. Rugs and furniture were sitting out in the mud-scummed lawn, airing out the stench of ripe flood water. The west side of the bridge, southeast of Bridgeport, was swept away, leaving the town inaccessible for people on that side of the county for many weeks to come. The only way to get into town until the bridge is fixed will be by rowing a boat across the river.

May 31

The pulverizing hailstorm last night finished off the wheat crop that the floods didn't get earlier. The Robbs, Robinsons, Montgomerys and I'm afraid many others, lost their entire crop. It was going to be a good yield this year, but not for Liberty Township now.

My flower beds and garden are flattened to an inch off the ground. I spent hours mulling over the loss of my first blooms as I cut back the stalks of my young plants. At least some of the flowers will fight back, pushing forth new growth and bursting in defiant bloom next month.

Mamma was worried about Christina in Salina. I wish we had one of those new telephones that you can hear people talking from miles away. Our last newspaper said that long distance telephoning is being planned to connect St. Paul, Minneapolis, Omaha, St. Louis and Kansas City together. Salina is going to be a connecting point for the central counties of Kansas. I wonder how long before Bridgeport will be connected to Salina.

June 7

Today's newspaper brought tales of disaster near and far and put our recent weather problems in perspective. On the 31st of May a cyclone touched down three times southwest of McPherson and Elyria, destroying farms. Luckily all families involved escaped injury by taking shelter in their storm cellars.

A Pacific mail steamer landing in San Francisco brought reports of a thousand homes devoured by fire in Japan, rendering 10,000 homeless, after an eruption took place on Oshima Island, destroying half the island.

Several columns of the paper were devoted to the horrible floods that happened in Johnstown, Pennsylvania, on the 3rd. A dam broke at the foot of a lake and washed out every town in the V-shaped valley. Johnstown was 18 miles from the start of the flood. Stories of how houses were floating down the river, with the inhabitants clinging to the roof and screaming for help, gave me chills. Thousands of people drowned in the cruel waters of the flood. Accounts from people that survived tell of piles of people caught in the uprooted trees and crushed lumber that were once buildings. I'm sick to my stomach after reading the accounts of this disaster. What must the people who have relatives living in that area be thinking?

June 15

Mamma's 45th birthday. Taking a break from our daily routine to do something special was weclomed by all of us.We celebrated by attending the ice cream social at Hessler's grove in Assaria this evening. The benefit for the formation of the Assaria band brought out a big crowd. Everyone is still talking about the Johnstown flood. Three carloads of flour from Salina will be sent to the flood victims.

June 25

Peter, Willie and Alfred have started binding wheat. The fields are spotty because of the storms we had this spring and rust disease, but at least we do have some wheat to harvest. They came home this evening, covered with the dark red specks of the rust, making them look like moving statues of red sandstone. Even Alfred's straw-blonde hair was tinted a dull red.

July 4

We talked Peter into taking the day off from harvest since we all wanted to partake of the festivities at Assaria. It was Julia's fifth birthday two days ago and we had promised to celebrate it on the 4th. After the firing of the anvil, the parade started down the center of town. I liked the Liberty wagon the best. Forty-two girls rode on it representing the 42 states of the union with Hattie Smith posed as 'Miss Liberty.' After the dust from the parade settled, we quenched our thirst by tasting the new soda water on tap at the drug store.

It was a beautiful day for the ceremonies held in the grove. Professor Andreen of Lindsborg gave the Swedish address and Dr. Knox read the Declaration of Independence. The Honorable J.R. Burton of Abilene captivated the audience with his eloquence and wisdom. Assaria baseball team won the $10 purse with their unbelievable 50 to 10 victory over Salemsborg. The runners up did receive a new ball and bat for their efforts though. Tom Dickey won in the sack race and Wilber Hopkins the egg race. They both received a dollar prize. Musical notes drifted around town as the Assaria Band played on and off throughout the day. There was a platform dance later tonight, but we didn't stay for that.

July 12

Kerr's threshing crew is here this week to thresh the wheat. Mamma, Carrie and I have been busy cooking for the extra men. I have lost count of the number of pies and cakes I have made. The flour bin in the kitchen cupboard has been refilled twice this week and it holds 20 pounds of flour. My only break has been to draw up butter or cream crocks from the well. Standing over the opening I get a hint of cool breeze rising from the depth of the bottom water.

The men were saying that Mr. Talbot in Assaria was buying wheat at 55 cents per bushel. Even when they take a break from farming, the men still talk about it.

July 20

There is going to be a general store in the new town that is located two miles east of us on Amos Hall's land. Johnson and Lindh, who have a store in Assaria, are opening up the branch store the first part of August. The area was named Hallville by the railroad when the railroad station was built in '87. So far there is just the depot, its stockyards and the post office stuck out in the middle of the prairie. I don't know if the store can make it without the usual cluster of houses that make up a town. We get our mail at Bridgeport and Mamma likes the selection at Swain's new grocery store, so we'll still do most of our trading there. But when we have bad weather or don't want to go around the river bends to cross the bridge, the Hallville store will be handy.

August 2

Today's newspaper reports forest fires raging near Boise City, Idaho, severe storms and floods in Chicago, and a fire in Wichita destroying $170,000 worth of property.

I also noticed the new large advertisement for Bethany College. Fall term starts September 17th. Tuition, board, room, furniture, fuel and light cost $3.00 a week. I wish I could go there a year, but Mamma and Peter think that's a lot of money, and that country schooling is enough for us children. I know Willie really wanted to go for more education, but our parents said no.

August 29

Mamma planned our fall shopping for dress material at Lindsborg today so we could attend the Harvest Home Picnic in the new Bethany Park. Dinner was sold on the grounds for 25 cents to help pay the debt of the park. The campus is so beautiful with the big brick buildings and the tree lined streets. I hope the students realize how lucky they are to get the chance to expand their knowledge.

Harvest in the garden will be in full swing at home soon. Rows of jelly jars and canned fruit already line half the shelves in the cellar from our work this summer. As the nights grow cooler, the rest of the garden crops will be plucked from the vine or uprooted from the earth. Packed in straw in wooden bins below the house, the vegetables will wait to become a meal this winter.

October 4

Read the advertisement in the newspaper for the annual Fall Festival in Lindsborg that is this next week. Since the roads have been so muddy, and we were in Lindsborg in August, I know we won't be going.

Also mentioned was that the ladies of McPherson are preparing for the chrysanthemum show this fall. Someday I hope to travel to McPherson to see the flower show. I have several mounds of gold and lavender mums in my garden, but their autumn display would pale against the vast exhibit in McPherson.

Johnson and Lindh's store in Hallville didn't last long. I rode Bonnie, our Indian pony, to the store for a spool of thread today and found out they are in the process of moving the merchandise to the old Ensle building in Bridgeport. I hope someone else eventually tries merchandising in Hallville again. We found the store very handy.

October 18

The *Assaria Argus* had a full report of the Sunday School Convention that we missed two days ago on account of the recent rains. Dr. Swensson from Bethany College, one of the featured speakers, didn't get to Assaria either because of the muddy roads.

John Ekstrand, the young Bridgeport druggist, was listed as having died of consumption last Sunday. He had been sick for some time. I wonder if he tried Dr. King's New Discovery, the medicine that is advertised to cure consumption and other ails. If a druggist can't cure himself, I don't have much faith in the medicine.

What really caught my eye was the article about the King of Sweden sending 300 volumes of his own books as a gift to the Bethany College Library. I wish I could borrow some of those books to read here at home this winter when we're homebound by the weather.

November 8

I was ready to take a break when Peter came back from town with this week's newspaper. I had just finished cleaning out the crock after churning and molding the new butter into blocks for this weekend's cooking. Pouring a glass of fresh buttermilk, I sat down and scanned the headlines.

Today's paper had an article about the McCoy and Hatfield vendetta that has ballooned into a small-scale war in West Virginia. Two hundred and fifty Hatfield men have armed their group with ten wagon loads of guns and ammunition to eradicate the McCoys. The paper mentioned talk of the governor calling in government troops to stop the war, but it was feared that with all the hiding places the families knew in the hills, the troops would be shot down by either or both sides of the feuding parties.

Other news was that the Dakota territory has been divided into North and South today and admitted as states. Montana and Washington were also admitted this week.

November 19

Smoke billowed in the gray morning sky to the northeast of us as we finished the chores today. It reminded me of the prairie fires that glowed in the distant night when I was little. Willie saddled horses, and he, Peter and Alfred took off with shovels in hand. A spark from the train engine had started the fire. Land was scorched for three and a half miles before the fire was put out. Willie said there were over 20 neighbors working on the blaze. The Vermillions and McVitties lost most of their stacked hay crop. Mamma sighed with relief when her men returned home. With a blaze that size, the wind can change direction and trap the fighters to their death. Nothing but their weary eyes showed through their soot-smudged faces. Hat to boots on all of them were still almost smoldering from where sparks burned holes. They reeked of smoke, dirt and sweat.

November 23

Peter went to Wheeler School last night for a meeting to form a Farmer's Alliance group. The group opposes high interest rates, high protective tariffs and high railroad freight rates. There are already 700 members of the Alliance in the county now. I'm not sure Peter agrees with everything that was discussed last night, but the farmers must stick together.

December 2

Last night two masked robbers entered Thomas Corrigan's home, three miles northeast of us. One of the men pointed a revolver and demanded "Your money or your life!" They tied him up and stole two $20 gold pieces, a $20 bill, his watch and a box of matches. It took Mr. Corrigan an hour to untie himself. Peter thinks the robbers are probably out of the county by now, but it still makes me uneasy. The shotgun is hanging above the back door, in case we need to protect ourselves. Us older children were taught how to shoot at an early age.

December 9

Tonight I went with the Granquists to the Christmas Bazaar at Bethany College. There was a large crowd since Governor Humphrey was the main speaker. With the Bethany Orchestra playing Christmas music, and decorated cookies piled high on the refreshment tables to sample, everyone was in a festive mood. Minnie Granquist and I studied the handwork of the holiday articles that were for sale in the booths. Our time together is limited, so we have spent spare moments together at her farm or mine this month. Best friends since before I can remember, Minnie and I will be world's apart soon. The Flensbergs, who have a grocery store in Bridgeport, are moving to Kansas City. They decided there wasn't enough opportunity for their boys in a small community so they plan to open up a tailor shop in the bigger city. They have hired Minnie to go with them to take care of their little girl, Edith, while Mrs. Flensberg works in the shop with her husband. I'll miss not having Minnie to confide in when I'm unsure about things.

December 13

While the stars still shown in the sky early this morning I crept down the stairs to the cold kitchen and stoked the stove to bring it to life. I'm sure Mamma heard me filling the coffee pot even though I was trying to be extra quiet. She must have remembered what day was today, because she didn't stir from her warm bed. After the coffee had cooked and I arranged a plate of rolls and cups, I started the Christmas season by waking the family up with St. Lucia's song and serving them coffee in bed. According to the medieval legend, St. Lucia, dressed in white with a crown of glowing candles encircling her head, fed the poor and hungry. Accused of witchcraft, St. Lucia was burned at the stake on December 13th, the shortest day of the year. To honor her memory, the oldest daughter of the family has the privilege of serving food to her family, but since Christina has moved away, it's my turn to uphold the tradition.

December 14

Peter was reading clips out loud from the *Assaria Argus* after supper tonight.

"This year's broomcorn harvest in McPherson County, covering 4000 acres, produced 1500 tons. The average price at $70 a ton is more profitable than corn at 17 cents a bushel or wheat at 50 cents a bushel."

"Jefferson Davis, the Confederate president, was buried this week in New Orleans. Thousands of people were present as his body paraded the streets."

"Stelson's in Falun is advertising they need girls to pick 300 chickens for market next week." He wanted to know if I wanted a ride over to Falun for the job, but I think I can find work closer to home to do. That's a lot of feathers to pluck!

December 24

After putting Julia and Mabel to bed last night, Peter dragged the cedar tree that had been stashed on the porch earlier in the evening, into the parlor to be decorated. An hour later, the scrawny evergreen cut from the river bank glowed with glass ornaments and homemade decorations. This evening after the dishes were washed from our *Julafton smörgåsbord*, the parlor door opened to reveal the brilliant Christmas tree. Peter had slipped into the parlor to light the candles while we kept the little girls occupied. Opening our presents this year was a challenge since Mabel wanted to help rip the paper off of every gift. She had as much fun with the wrapping as her presents.

To finish our Christmas Eve celebration we traveled to the Bridgeport Church for their special program "The Arctic Excursion." After the program, the ushers handed out paper sacks of hard candy and nuts to the children as we left the church. Even though I'm too old to be counted as a child, Mr. Perrill winked and handed me a sack. As I eat the ribbon candy this week, I'll think of him.

1890

Finishing the House

January 1

I pray we have a bountiful and healthy year for our family. LaGrippe has made hundreds of people sick in Salina. I hope this Russian influenza doesn't spread to Liberty Township. Mamma told Peter to get a large bottle of the best cure available when he's in Larson's drugstore this week. With medicine and a doctor in town, Mamma doesn't worry to the frantic point about us children when we become sick now. In her early homesteading days, no doctor or medicine was available when a disease or accident befell a member of the family. All she had were herbs in her prairie garden to concoct a tea or salve to attempt to soothe the pain. It seemed like the first section of the Assaria graveyard had a new grave dug every time we went to church when it was first started. Parents could lose all their children in a short week if a contagious disease filtered into their home. Thank goodness for modern medicine.

January 6

Carrie and Alfred are back in school after Christmas vacation. Alfred was needed for the fall field work, so this is his first day of the school year. I imagine the teacher had several older boys start today. They fit in what schooling they can between the crop cycles on the land.

Carrie's armload of books landed with a thud on the kitchen table as soon as she got home this afternoon. The new books the school board ordered had arrived and Carrie had permission to bring them home overnight. There aren't enough copies for each child in the school, but the books will circulate home to each family so the parents get the chance to see what their children are studying. This evening after supper we each took a book to read. Willie thumbed through Harper's Geography, Alfred seriously studied Fisher's Arithmetic and I read Barne's History. Carrie copied words from the Hartington's Speller and Peter, with Julia and Mabel crowded on his lap, read out loud from the Barne's Reader. We speak mostly Swedish at home, so Peter likes to read English to the girls to get them ready for school.

January 18

Clouds of frozen breath rose from the feed bunk this morning as the cattle nudged into their spot at the wood-sided feeder. Their winter white-crusted coats cracked in miniature valleys down the sides of their necks as they moved around to keep warm in the frosty twelve degrees below zero weather. At midmorning a caravan of nine immigrant wagons passed by our place going south. Numbing cold and frostbite must surely be traveling with them.

Snuggling up to the stove tonight I caught up on the newspapers. There were two fires recently in Salina. Curry's drugstore on the corner of Santa Fe and Iron was burned out, and Jewett's livery barn on Santa Fe burned down on the 9th. With this sub zero weather, there would be no way to efficiently fight blazes. Water thrown near the flames would turn into treacherous ice to hinder the efforts of the firemen.

I doubt we'll go to church tomorrow. Chores takes so much longer in such cold weather. Ice has to be broken out of the water tank for the cattle to drink, snow scooped out of the feed bunks before the feed is poured in for the animals and so forth. Sunday School is always suspended in January due to the low attendance with the bad weather.

Last Sunday morning our bedroom window was so frosted over I couldn't see out. Only a white blur met my eyes in the pre-dawn light. The whipping of the wind told my ears that we were having a snow storm, so a trip to church was out of the question. We're not supposed to do work on Sunday but God's creation of winter storms sure puts that theory to the test. After struggling through the storm to do the morning chores, we had devotions after dinner.

Bundled up in extra clothing, we trooped into the cold parlor last Sunday afternoon to dismantle the Christmas tree. The Swedish Christmas season ends on the 13th, St. Knut's Day, so Mamma decided to take down the decorations a day early to give us something to do since we were house bound. And it was Peter's 36th birthday so we wanted to do something special. Mamma carefully wrapped her glass balls as we plundered the tree, eating all the edible ginger cookie ornaments we found hidden among the branches. Traditionally all the Christmas food is supposed to last until St. Knut's Day, but I think it was all devoured the week before except what was decorating the tree. When the tree was stripped bare, Mamma opened the parlor door shouting the traditional Swedish saying "Out with the Yule!" to end the Christmas season, and Peter tossed the tree into the swirling blizzard.

January 27

My 17th birthday. Looking back, another year has passed without much change in my life except the seasons. Mamma suggested we set the quilting frame up in the parlor to start quilting the top I finished recently. I didn't use any particular pattern on this quilt. Patches of material from the scrap basket were randomly sewed to scatter the colors throughout the quilt. I embroidered different types of stitching around each piece, using leftover colored thread from various projects. As we stretched the backing, batting and pieced top on the frame, Julia pointed to the different patches and named whose old dress it once was.

January 31

This afternoon I hiked over to visit Laura Robinson who has been recovering from a bout of tonsillitis. I could have ridden Bonnie, but I felt like stretching my legs. With my extra layers of winter petticoats and my lined cloak, I almost worked up a sweat walking that mile and a half.

I brought my Vick's Floral Guide for her to read this week. It's a hundred pages of flower and vegetable seeds that I've spent hours poring over since it arrived in the mail. Mamma got the new Pinney and Long Nursery Catalog from Ellsworth in the mail today but I couldn't take it because she wants to look at it before it circulates around the neighborhood. Laura let me borrow her new Montgomery

Wards catalog. This big issue has everything imaginable available. All one has to do is send in their order and money, and the merchandise will be delivered to the person's post office.

On the way home I stopped by the Olsons to see the new baby born yesterday. Hannah and baby Gottfrid Emanuel are doing fine. A day sooner and he could have shared his birthday with our state, Kansas, which turned 29 Wednesday.

February 13

O. J. Thorstenberg, a mile west of Assaria had a farm sale today. Since the weather has been nice lately, the roads are drying out and we can get around the neighborhood again. I think these sales become informal meetings of the Farmer's Alliance. The men come home with all kinds of news. They heard of the latest bulletin put out by the Kansas State Agricultural College on pig feeding. I'm sure Willie will send for it.

On the way home, they stopped in Assaria to trade butter for supplies. The general store is buying butter at 14 cents a pound this month. After checking out J. O. Johnson's new hardware store that just opened for business, they stopped at the Freeman House for coffee. Peter said it looks good inside after being renovated this winter.

February 15

The Star Literary meeting had a valentine theme tonight. The crowd was in a festive mood with the school children's heart creations still decorating the walls. Tonight's topic of debate was humorous instead of the usual serious one. All the young women brought special treats for refreshments. I baked and decorated a cake for my contribution. On top of the frosting I arranged drained canned cherries in a heart shape. I have no special valentine in my life, but I got a pretty card in the mail from Minnie. Her social life seems to be expanding as she meets new friends in Kansas City.

March 5

I wasn't surprised by the dusting of snow we received last night. It's been so cold the last several days it is hard to believe it's March. At least with this late freeze people could finish getting the ice out of the river. The boys have been cutting and hauling ice out of the Smoky

Hill River to be stored in the Bridgeport ice house. I'll remember their hard work when we make ice cream this summer.

Willie, Alfred and I spent this evening at the Youth's Cornet Band Concert held in the Assaria Music Hall. It was their final performance for their first year. My favorite song from the program was "Stars of the Twilight," a duet sung by A. J. Thorstenberg and J. O. Johnson. After the concert we went to the Freeman house, where the band served cake and coffee. It was a clear bright night to ride home in.

March 17

The weather has changed so fast. Warm breezes are now penetrating into our country air and the peach buds are starting to swell. The moss on the north side of the house is like a emerald velvet carpet, growing thicker each day as the temperature warms up. Willie plowed the garden, and I've spent the week cutting up sprouted potatoes that we've been saving in the cellar for spring planting. I relished the sensation of sun-warmed soil as I stick the potato eyes into the newly turned soil. Although she laughs about it now, Mamma told what a chore it used to be to plant the garden by herself the first years with us little ones helping her. But after the hard winter everyone wanted out of the dugout to soak up the spring sunshine.

March 28

We spent the afternoon at Star School for the end-of-year picnic. Albertina Almquist and I situated ourselves on a quilt and caught up on all the gossip of the neighborhood while we feasted on the best of the neighborhood women's recipes.

Mabel, who just turned two yesterday, chased after the young children who played hide'n seek while the older ones played baseball. We sadly reminisced how one of our classmates was killed when we were playing the hiding game when we were in school. He dropped on his knees in the tall grass, landed on a rattlesnake and was fatally bitten. Now the school grounds are mowed and the surrounding prairie sod has been broken into crop fields. There are still plenty of snakes around, but they tend to stay in the prairie grass where they feel protected.

The men nearby talked about the jump in the price of wheat. It is selling for 86 cents per bushel in Kansas City.

Someone had been over to Brookville to see the destruction from the fire that burned the downtown on the 14th. A whole block, ten businesses including the post office, were wiped out that night.

It was mentioned that Gypsum City might be building two more stucco mills. The present mill grinds 60 tons of stucco out of gypsum rock a day. Their product is shipped all over the nation to plaster walls in new buildings.

April 2

All hopes to attend the *Messiah* performance at Bethany College tonight were dashed with today's downpour. This annual event in Lindsborg has become very popular since it started eight years ago. People around here associate the *Messiah* with the Easter season.

The roads will be a mucky mess for the rest of the week. If one attempts the draw across the creek going west of Granquists, you're liable to get the buggy buried up to its axel because you never hit bottom. I tried to cross it last spring, got stuck and tried to help the horse by pushing the back wheels. I ended up face first in the murky mess, mud plastered down the entire front of my dress, from the white lace collar to the hem. I had to unhitch the horse from the buggy, ride back to Mr. Granquist's farm and ask him to help me out. His team of draft horses pulled the mud-caked buggy out of the hole for me without much effort. That was one of the rare occasions I wished I lived in town instead of the country.

April 11

The roads have dried up enough that Alfred and I brought the butter to Assaria this morning. Kitchen staples like sugar and salt, and kerosene for the glass lanterns replaced the blocks of butter in the back of the wagon.

Uncle Frank Fager came out of the newspaper printers as we went by, so we stopped to talk. He and Uncle Andrew Johnson bought an imported Clydesdale stallion recently and they had horse bills printed up to advertise stud services this spring. Everyone has at least three or four pairs of draft horses on their farm to do the farm work. Farmers breed the mares for new stock each year and need a stallion if they don't have one of their own. These towering beasts have replaced the slow oxen teams on most homesteads when the farmer could afford the horses.

April 16

Took a break from the housework today and attended the Saline County Sunday School Convention at our church. Good weather meant a large crowd of families to hear the programs. We said our goodbyes to Pastor Kjellgren. He has resigned because of his ill health. After their household goods sale on Friday, the family will move out of the parsonage. So far the church council has had no luck calling a new pastor to take his place.

Passing through the downtown, we noticed that Miss Hannah Olson's new millinery store was open. Of course we had to go in to see what was new for spring. No lady goes off the farm without the proper hat and gloves.

April 25

Gentle sprinkles broke my concentration while I was beating the dirt out of the parlor rug, so I had to quit and lug it back inside. We're hitting spring cleaning with a vengeance. Yesterday we washed windows: Mamma inside, while I was outside on the same window. Of course the streaks were always on my side. Peter came from the neighbors telling us that Anna Stenfors had a new baby named John Aron this morning. The passing rain just sprinkled down the dust on the roads, so Mamma took some food up to the Stenfors' late this afternoon. After she left, I took a break and wrote in my diary.

May 8

Dangerous winds that came up this noon kept us worried since the boys had gone to town this morning. Billowing like a mad bull, the blasts crashed down several large limbs from our shade trees. A gust caught the barn door and blew it off the hinges, sailing in the air for a moment until it crashed in the dirt. Willie and Alfred waited out the gale at the Assaria elevator and told how the wind ripped the smoke stack off the elevator while they were there! If they hadn't had a full load of bundled shingles in the wagon, I think they would have tipped over coming home.

May 15

The summer kitchen on the west side of the house is almost finished. The shingles are nailed down and the boys almost have all the siding on. This lean-to attached to the kitchen will be used for everything from separating cream to thawing frozen muddy boots, besides cooking our meals during the summer months. This is the fourth addition on to the original stone one-room house, not counting adding on the porches.

Uncle Ola Peterson was out today to give us an estimate on paint for the whole house. Mamma wants to paint it a light yellow with cream, yellow and green trim. I'm sure we'll do the painting, but she wanted to give Ola the paint sale.

May 17

Mamma and us sunbonneted girls went to Assaria today to buy some dress fabric and deliver eggs. Hanson and Trulson's Dry Goods Store buys eggs for nine cents a dozen. Mamma brought in two wooden crates holding 15 dozen each, so we got $2.70 worth of calico and gingham material in exchange for our eggs. At eight cents a yard, we got almost thirty-five yards of fabric.

Mamma gave me money for lemonade for us four girls at the Freeman House while she had the doctor check her aching tooth. She ended up getting it pulled so I drove home and Carrie and I cooked supper tonight. I hope I don't have bad teeth when I get old.

May 27

Light early summer breezes wafted through the Bridgeport festivities for Decoration Day today. The Assaria Band performed a rousing concert in the open air of the park. I savored the first taste of this year's ice cream as we watched the Assaria baseball team beat Bridgeport 25 to 5.

The town has steadily grown over the past years. Downtown supports several stores, two hotels, the Presbyterian church and the school. The elevator is sandwiched in between the two railroad depots and their stockyards. The cheese factory and the mill are the biggest industries in town. The only drawback to this town exploding in size is the threat of floods being situated right on the river.

The area around Bridgeport has become so populated that part of our township gets its mail at the Wonderly Post Office that is dropped off at the Hallville railroad station. The dividing line is at our north corner. While we go to Bridgeport for our mail, Olsons collect theirs at Wonderly. I once asked why it wasn't called the

Hallville Post Office. The reason is there was once a post office in McPherson County called that name for a short time in '84.

May 30

We've received our very last issue of the *Assaria Argus*. Dursley Sargent has decided to quit printing the Assaria newspaper. We'll miss our local news. Peter has subscribed to the *Salina Sun* to take the *Argus'* place. But now we won't get such detailed reports of the Assaria and Bridgeport area.

June 4

Charles Everhart was here today to take the 1890 census. Besides who is living on this land, the government has a list of 32 questions about what we raise on the farm. The newspaper had listed the questions last month, so Peter and Mamma had tallied the numbers of acres of each crop, how many animals and fowl, etc., and were ready for the census taker. He stayed for dinner since they finished the questionnaire around noon time. Whoever is around the farm at mealtime is always welcome and encouraged to stay.

July 3

Two new states of the Union will be celebrating the 4th of July tomorrow. Idaho was admitted as a state to the union yesterday and Wyoming will be admitted the 10th.

Willie was plowing fire guards before noon around the cut wheat field by the school house when Prince and King stopped suddenly and refused to budge. Walking in front of the horses, the whir of rattles stopped him in his tracks. A den of rattlesnakes lay in the path of the plow. The horses knew that danger was ahead and were smart enough to stop. After clubbing the rattlers to death and throwing them out of the horses' path, they finished plowing.

Willie's morning episode made me pause this afternoon as I headed for the pasture to bring in the milk cows. This time of year when the sun goes down late, the cows sometimes balk at coming to the barn to be milked. Mamma's stick still stands in the corner of the kitchen by the back door, so I took it for protection. She's killed many snakes with that club.

September 8

Since Julia turned six this summer she tagged along with Carrie today for her first day at school. She is very shy and worried about doing her lessons right. Several other little neighbor girls started today also. Cousin Emelia Johnson, Emma Olson and Hilda Mattson were a few who she already knows well in her new class. Cousin Millie Johnson started last year, so Julia shared a desk with her. We've taught her the alphabet and numbers in English, so she has a head start. Seems strange with only Mabel home with Mamma and me.

November 19

Tonight Willie, Alfred and I went to the masquerade supper held at the Mills building at Bridgeport. I wore a handmade mask over my eyes, but my dandelion yellow hair and my 5'2" height gave away my identity. Besides, everyone knows my good dress and hat. At least with the mask on it was easier to spy on the boy I have a crush on. Unfortunately, he was flirting with another girl.

Most of Bridgeport was present with several buggy loads from Liberty and Smoky View Townships. The majority of the farmers have their fall jobs done and it was time to have a little fun.

This last week we have been busy butchering our meat for the winter. The boys slaughtered the animals and cut up the meat, then we fried down the meat and packed it in crocks, sealing the top with hot lard to keep the meat from spoiling. After the hams are done soaking in brine water and smoked for four weeks, they are hung in the cellar. When we need to fix ham for a meal, we cut off a hunk and cook it.

Tomorrow we'll make soap from the lard and stove ashes. Thank goodness Mamma now buys a soap for our baths. The homemade soap scrubs the clothes clean, but it's harsh on skin.

December 15

Peter went to a Farmer's Alliance meeting tonight. Members were concerned that hogs are selling at a low $3 per hundred weight, wheat has dropped to 74 cents a bushel and corn 55 cents a bushel.

He came home with the news that there has been an outbreak of diphtheria and chicken pox in Lindsborg and scarlet fever in McPherson this month. Men were warned to keep their families out of McPherson County if possible.

1891

Sister Portraits

January 1

The New Year's Eve party was spoiled last night for me when I heard the news of the Indian massacre on Wounded Knee Creek in South Dakota this week. Here we were celebrating the start of a new year, while the future of the native people of America looks very bleak.

Our government has been pushing the Indian tribes into unsettled land for several years until it has gotten to the point where most of the Plains Indians are now living on reservations. Because the government agents are telling them to start farming, convert to Christianity and send their children to school, several tribes had sought condolence in the revived Indian religion called Ghost Dance. For some, the chanting and singing while dancing in a circle, brought visions of their dead relatives in the after world. The visions promised a new world full of buffalo herds, return of their dead and the vanishing of the white men. To many tribes, the Ghost Dance was a release of frustration. Ghost shirts and dresses of white cloth painted with symbols were thought to provide protection, even from bullets of their enemies. The Indian Bureau of Affairs saw this dance as an imminent prelude to an Indian uprising.

Last Monday, the army surrounded and attempted to disarm a Sioux Indian village. Uneasy because Sitting Bull was killed last week by government agents, the leader advanced forward with a white flag. While some of the soldiers were confiscating guns from the camp, a gun misfired and both sides jumped into action. When the Indians, including women and children, broke through the first line of soldiers to escape, they were gunned down by rapid-firing Hotchkiss guns. Photographs in the newspaper I saw at the party showed frozen corpses laying everywhere. Because this army group was from Custer's Seventh Cavalry, it was commented that they wanted revenge against the Indians. This last battle seals the doom of the Indian's life on their prairie.

When the first settlers arrived in Liberty Township, they lived compatibly with the Indians, even though they were wary of each other. Mamma always shared whatever she was cooking or baking with our native neighbors if they came to our door asking for food. I remember us children hiding under the bed when we saw the strangers. Christina remembers two young Indians spending the night in our house when the weather was bad. Papa put their horses and guns in the barn and invited them to stay. The next morning after breakfast they left with extra food Mamma had given them.

January 9

The sun appeared as a fuzzy white dot trying to pierce the fog today. The neighborhood was quiet except for the revved-up train breaking through drifts of snow as it whistled through our land. The snowdrifts around the township have blocked anyone from traveling. Steam rose from the milk pail this morning as I emptied the cow's udder. The only reason the cats left their cozy dens in the haymow in such cold weather was for their morning squirt of hot fresh milk. With so many animals vying for the stream, half of them get soaked in the process, but they lick each other off in a hurry, not wanting to waste a drop. Trix and Babe, our bay Belgian team, were frisky this morning trying to work off the cooped up energy they've felt in the barn stalls. They were impatient to get hitched up and start their morning work. With the road blade, snow had to be removed from the yard before the feed wagon could get down the alley. Seems like the biggest drifts are always in the worst spots.

January 27

For my 18th birthday I went back to school—for the day. The pupils are studying the Civil War, so Mr. Lapsley held the floor today. Every year he returns to retell the stories of the war and slave life he escaped from, and none of us tire of his storytelling. He was born on a plantation in Kentucky, but because of the approaching battle fronts of the war, he moved with his master to Missouri and later Texas. When Mr. Lapsley was going to be sold to a man he didn't want to work for, he and his cousin ran off. Within three days they were captured by Southern-sympathizing Indians. Escaping a month later by himself in a rain storm, Mr. Lapsley endured the Indian's five-day hunt for their prisoner. Two days were spent in the cover of a willow tree in neck-deep river water. When the Indians were above him on the river bank, he slipped under water, breathing through a hollow reed stem. To this day, Mr. Lapsley can't wear shoes because of the damage done to his feet standing in freezing water. No matter what time of year, he wears rubber galoshes instead of boots.

I invited him over for a piece of birthday cake after school. With Julia and Mabel's attention, he told more stories between bites of cake and sips of coffee.

March 20

Glancing out the kitchen window this afternoon, I thought I spied bits of color fluttering in the sky. Looking again I realized it was kite flying day at school. One project the children look forward to is the chance to fly their homemade kites on the first windy day of spring. Some years the weather doesn't cooperate because of rain or no wind, but today's gusts were a challenge.

Simple paper and wooden sticks make up the kite, but color comes into play when the children raid their mother's scrap basket for bits of bright fabric for the tails. I took Mabel to the top of the railroad tracks where we had a panoramic view of the sky. The kites dipped and swirled in the wind, some crashing and a few staying aloft until the end of recess.

April 10

I hope the proverb "April cold and wet fills the barn and barrel" comes true so we aren't wasting this month due to miserable weather. We can't turn the ground or plant in this soggy soil that drips when you squeeze a handful of mud.

On one warm day last month I did get the dead winter material raked out of the flower beds. The peonies haven't shown their maroon curled stalks yet, but I know the new rosettes flat to the ground are the wild white yarrow Mamma dug out of the prairie years ago. The asters, purple ironweed and prairie coneflowers come up every year from the roots. Creamy yellow butter-and-eggs, which look similar to snapdragons, sprout each year from the seed that burst from the seed pods each fall. Any day now the dense mat of pussy toes will shoot up their two-inch high mass of fuzzy seven-toed flowers. Admiring these spring flowers requires me to get down on my knees and peer close to them.

The early batch of baby chicks haven't wandered much past the fringe of their mother's feathered breast since they hatched. The chickens' dour mood shows they hate this weather, while the ducks stretch their necks and flap their wings in the rain, loving the raindrops running off their feathers.

May 15

We had a lightning rod salesman stop by the farm today. Wiping her floured hands on her apron to shake his hand, Mamma was polite, but wouldn't let him in the door. Mamma used to handle Indians and roving cowboys in her homestead days so this man wasn't getting past her. There have been reports of fraud concerning these salesman in the newspaper lately.

After hand kneading enough dough for our needed supply of bread, I was ready to spend the afternoon in the garden while Mamma baked the dozen loaves in the hot kitchen. Last month's rain has produced a bumper crop of tiny weeds that seem to double in size overnight. I threw the larger weeds in a bushel basket to give to the chickens. When I tossed the wilting plants in the pen, the chickens squawk and feathers fly, but as soon as they realize what it is, they attack with vengeance, fighting for each peck of fresh greens they can get. One rooster had other ideas. More than once today the ornery thing was chasing Mabel around the farm yard. If he keeps it up, he'll be next Sunday's chicken dinner.

June 15

Mamma's 47th birthday. Us children put our money together and ordered her a subscription to *Ladies Home Journal*. She prefers to read Swedish, but has learned to read English while helping us with our schoolwork. Besides the articles, I study the illustrations to decipher the new fashions in women's clothing.

Aunt Marie and Uncle Andrew stopped for coffee on their way home from town. The men commented that wheat harvest is going to be light weight and low grade due to a combination of Hessian fly, chinch bugs and black rust. It is so disheartening to sow, tend and pray for a good crop to feed your family, and then end up with very little. Mamma seems to take it in stride. When Peter harps about the bad crop, she reminds him of the grasshopper plague of '74 that wiped out every bit of crop, fruit and green substance in Kansas. We literally had nothing to eat that year.

They also told the shocking news about the earthquakes that nearly destroyed Northern Italy last week, toppling solid stone buildings and crushing people in the rubble. I can't imagine the ground shaking below your feet. At least with a Kansas tornado, you can usually tell it's coming by the change of weather and take shelter in the cellar.

July 4

Spent the day harvesting wheat instead of celebrating Independence Day. Since we had so much rain last week, we haven't been able to get into the fields until now. It will be a poor crop, but we must harvest it before something else happens to it. Carrie's fresh squeezed lemonade and my *smörbakelser* were greatly appreciated when we brought refreshments out to the wheat field this afternoon. Sitting in the shade cast by the wagons we reminisced about past fourth of July celebrations.

Supper laid out on old quilts was eaten by the whole family in the field tonight. With daylight lasting until after nine, the men will work until dark. For a special treat for the holiday, I dug new potatoes to add to the creamed peas for supper.

We talked about the letter I received yesterday from Minnie, describing the rains they have had in Kansas City. This week's newspaper told of the city flooding. Since this letter was postmarked several days ago, I wonder if she is in the flooded area. If we were at the celebration today, I could have asked Minnie's parents if they had any more news. Since their buggy didn't go by our farm, I imagine they are harvesting today too.

August 8

Carrie and I hurried through our evening chores as fast as the cows would let us. Mrs. Mary McPhail started her music class in Bridgeport tonight and we didn't want to be late. As I tugged the cow's tit to get the last drop of milk out, the cow deposited fresh manure on her tail and then swung it at the flies bothering her. The tail smacked my head, smearing the manure into my hair. Carrie poured a bucket of cold well water over my head to wash the worst of it out. Soaping the smell out of my hair delayed our leaving and we rode pell mell to town. At least with my waist-length hair flying in the air, it was dry by the time we reached Bridgeport. I rolled it up quickly into a bun as we ran up the stairs of the school. Out of breath, we slid into back seats just as the group was finishing the first song.

August 24

The weather has been miserable the last two weeks for everyone. The pigs spend their whole day in their mud wallow without moving. Standing in the shade of the barn, the horses stand opposite each other, using their tails to swish the flies out of each other's face. If the heat wasn't so bad, I'd yell at the dog for scratching himself a hole in the flower bed along the north side of the house. But I can't blame him for wanting to lay his furry body on the damp ground where I threw the wash water this morning.

After the sweaty work of heating water and rubbing a mountain of clothes clean on the wash board, I was ready for a cool spot myself. My relief came by pouring a bucket of well water on the porch to scrub off the dust. As the cold water chilled the sun-warmed boards, my bare feet standing in the water did the same thing for my body.

Looking up from my job, I spied a tramp walking towards the house from the railroad tracks. In this weather, the poor soul must have been dehydrated to the point of sun stroke. After calling Mamma from the kitchen, I refilled the well bucket and offered the man the tin cup that always hangs on a hook on the well's windlass. He was dirty, but very polite and thankful for my gesture of kindness. Mamma won't let tramps in the house, but she made two big sandwiches for him to eat while he sat under the front shade tree to rest.

He was wanting work, but Mamma told him we weren't doing any field work until it rains again.

The ground is so hard from the hot weather that Peter can't get the plow into the ground. Two months ago we thought the ground would never dry up. Both farmers and gardeners are grumbling about the bad weather this summer.

September 18

As a special trip for the girls before school starts next week, we rode the train from Bridgeport to Salina for the Sell's Circus Show. The big canvas tents were bursting with people, gasping as trained animals and trapeze artists performed death-defying acts. I don't think Mamma approved of everything we saw, but she clapped just as loud as the rest of us.

Cabinet Portrait Studio had a booth set up on the circus grounds to take photos, so we had our pictures taken before we went into the big tent. Julia and Mabel were in one picture and Carrie and I in another.

Alma and Carrie

October 10

I'm aching all over from the first day of harvesting corn. With four of us snapping the ears off the stalks, it won't take all winter, but my hands will be cracked and sore from the rough husks until they get used to it. Mamma is taking care of Mabel and the household work by herself for now. If the weather looks like it will turn bad, she'll bundle up Mabel, put her in the safety of the wagon and help with the harvest. Peter said corn is selling at 30 cents a bushel this week.

November 8

A Pastor Wistrand from McPherson has accepted the call to our church and will begin in December. We've been without a formal minister for over a year.

After church today we heard the results for the elections that were held last Tuesday for township seats. The results for Liberty were C. M. Verillion, trustee; D. A. Eagles, clerk; S. B. Young, treasurer and W. T. Montgomery and L. L. Thurman as constables.

When we were leaving town we drove by the vacant house south of the hotel that burned down Friday night. Luckily the wind was blowing from the southwest, or the business district would have burned too.

December 25

A light snow, like sugar crystals, powdered the roads last night. But instead of the threat of bad weather, we won't be going this morning to *Julotta,* our Christmas service at church, since LaGrippe is a serious threat in area towns now. With our big family we made our own choir to sing the Christmas anthem *Hosianna* before we sat down for breakfast.

Lighting the candles tonight on the *ljuskrona,* our Swedish candelabra that sits on the parlor table, brought back memories of early Christmases on the prairie. Papa carved the wooden branches, one arm for each of us, as we were born. The tradition stopped after Papa died, but we still light it on Christmas in remembrance of him.

1892

The New Granary

January 1

Ellis Island Immigrant Station officially opened in New York today. Pictures in the newspaper of the building look so grand. Thousands of people are moving to America and all of them will go past the Statue of Liberty and through this new station before they travel to their place of destination.

When my family came to New York, the ship first stopped at the Quarantine Station six miles below New York, which checked the health conditions of the ship's passengers. When arriving at the Castle Garden Immigrant Station, the passengers made their way into the Rotunda, a huge circular central hall. Mamma said it was so confusing and frightening with the crush of hundreds of people and different languages being spoken all around them. But agents were there to register them, figure out their destination and railroad tickets, exchange their money and send them on their way into the foreign world of America. Mamma said she was so relieved when she, Christina and Papa passed the health inspection and got out of there.

January 15

At thirteen degrees below zero, our wagon ride to the cemetery could have been much more bearable if we still had the old buffalo robes we used to wrap up in when we were little. The wool blankets we use now just don't cut the chilling wind. I don't think the weather seeped in the bodies of the bereaved though; their hearts are already cold today. Winter is a hard time to have a funeral. Chipping a grave out of the frozen dirt requires a pick axe and time. This morning trip was to say good-bye to Uncle Frank's 85-year-old mother, Ingrid Fager.

January 21

Alvira, Hannah and Pete Olson's month-old daughter died today. As her life started to flutter away, Mr. Olson galloped into town to retrieve Reverend Wikstrand. He needed to baptize Alvira before she died so her soul would live in heaven. The doctor had already been out but could not do anything for her body. He said Alvira would soon be in God's arms. This is the second child the Olsons have lost.

January 27

Since it is prayer week at church to strengthen the spiritual life of the congregation, I spent the evening of my 19th birthday at the revival. Luckily the weather cooperated, or we wouldn't have made it to any of the meetings. The town people think nothing of going every night, but they don't have five miles of dirt roads to travel.

We have subscribed to a new Lindsborg paper, the *Lindsborg Posten* written in Swedish by Dr. Swensson. It mostly tells of church and Bethany College news. It mentioned that Salemsborg Church plans to meet every night for six weeks.

February 29

The extra day every four years causes the bachelors to hide because on the 29th the women can ask the men to marry them. If I'm not married by the next leap year, maybe I'm ask someone!

April 5

We had poor attendance at the Star Literary tonight. Since it was the last meeting of the season and the weather was good, I guess the boys decided to skip the meeting and work late in the field. Corn planting is just around the corner. Alfred and Willie were still framing on the new granary when Carrie and I left for the meeting.

Rumors circulated around at the program that Smolan was blown away by a cyclone last week. Someone said that the Salemsborg community was hit, leaving many people homeless and destitute.

Since we're in the process of building a new granary, I'm glad the storm wasn't in our area. The stacks of lumber and shingles would have been blown to who knows where. Stormy weather off and on for the past week has put us on edge.

April 8

Went across the new bridge south of Bridgeport this evening on our way to the Ladies Mutual Aid supper. As we trotted across the bridge, I noticed a sign on it stating, "Five dollar fine for riding or driving over this bridge faster than a walk." I didn't spy anyone patrolling the bridge to enforce the law though.

May 1

Carrie's hardest studying for the spring is over. It was end-of-school tests last month and confirmation today at church. Carrie and classmate Emma Stenfors studied together several afternoons lately to quiz each other. Carrie walks northeast to her house, or Emma would walk here. Since I remember most of it by heart, I quizzed her as we stitched the trim on her confirmation dress this last week. Nearly the whole catechism book has to be memorized to give the correct answers to Pastor during the oral exam. With twenty-four in her class, it took a long time to question everyone.

June 16

If I'm not in the middle of a cherry tree picking fruit this week, I'm pitting the seeds, or sweating over the stove canning the dozens of jars of cherries we'll put up for the winter. Mamma made several cherry pies today and us girls walked down to Mr. Lapsley's this evening with one for him. We spent a blissful hour sitting on his porch steps, listening to his tales while he savored a piece of the juicy fresh pie.

July 29

The dusty aroma of newly threshed wheat mingles with the scent of fresh-milled lumber in the new granary. The men have worked on the building all spring and summer around their field work. The inside rooms were ready for the sacks of wheat filled by the threshing crew this week. There are two small grain bins on the east end of the building and a room the size of both on the west end for stacking sacks, tools and such. The main floor of the granary is built two feet high instead of ground level to protect the grain from rising water in the event of our occasional floods. On the north and south sides of the building, the steep-pitched roof slopes down to lean-to sheds to protect the wagons and implements from the elements. Instead of the expense of planking this part, the floor will just be dirt that will harden with use. The men installed sliding doors on both ends of the side sheds so equipment can be taken out from either way. Also, it's easier when we unload wagons of grain into the grain bins to loop out the other door than try to back the team and wagon out the way we came in. A cupola on top adds decoration only since Peter didn't want a hole in the roof above the open bins below where rain could leak in. Between now and plowing we hope to get the siding brushed with the gallons of red paint Peter bought a month ago. Each step seems to take longer than planned, but it will get done.

The new granary

August 26

Christina is here this week helping with the apple harvest. Besides needing apples for herself, she likes to be home to pick the apples off of her "Christmas apple" tree. Mr. Lapsley gave her an apple the first Christmas on the homestead, and the seeds planted from that apple produced this special tree. After spending part of each morning picking apples, we sort them by quality for different uses. The best blemish-free apples are stored in the cellar for fresh eating this winter. Several bushels are sliced and layered on cheese cloth-covered screens to dry into shriveled leather rings of dried fruit for *fruktsoppa* and pies. All day a pot of diced apples slowly simmers into apple butter. Whenever any of us walks by it, we pause to stir it to keep it from sticking.

With a heavy crop this year we had to buy more glass canning jars. Butter from our last three churnings were traded for Mason quart jars. At 90 cents a dozen, it took seven pounds of butter for each twelve jars to trade even.

The light yellow tint starting to show on the green pears means the last crop from the orchard will soon be ready. Cherries were picked in June and the peaches and apricots in July. Instead of plum trees planted in the orchard, we raid the wild plum thicket along the creek.

Relaxing on the east porch tonight, I noticed the colorful red dots of apples we saw Monday evening as we looked towards our orchard are almost gone now. Christina pulled my thoughts away from the harvest when she read out loud the advertisement in today's *Lindsborg News* about the 10th annual Kansas State Fair in Topeka, September 12-17. Swan will be going to see the new buggy equipment displayed at the fair and she might go with him. I've never been east past Salina, but someday I'll get out and see the rest of Kansas.

October 6

The Dalton outlaw gang, famous for robbing trains and banks in the Indian Territory, met their match yesterday morning as they tried to rob two banks simultaneously in Coffeeville, Kansas. A business man saw the five-member gang come out of an alley, split and enter two banks in the business district. Alarmed when he recognized one of them from wanted posters, the gentleman ran into a nearby store. Other townspeople witnessed the bank robberies through the plate glass windows of the two banks and joined him. Arming themselves with guns from the general store, the townspeople waited for the robbers to leave the banks. What followed was twelve minutes of shooting between the gang and the townspeople. When it ended, the marshal and four citizens of Coffeeville had given their lives to kill four of the five bank robbers. Store fronts with shattered glass and bloody floors from the wounded left the town in shock as they realized they had killed the famous Dalton gang.

November 14

We spent the day at Aunt Magda's to help butcher and preserve their winter supply of meat. After the cold weather prohibits the meat from spoiling, we move around to each family's house. With several people doing assigned tasks, the job goes much easier. I spent the afternoon peeling and cutting up potatoes. This mixture, with salt, pepper and allspice, is ground with the meat and stuffed in the cleaned pig intestines to make *potatiskorv*. Boiled, then fried in lard until crispy brown, it is one of our favorite meats for the Christmas season.

Politics was the topic at the dinner table at noon. Grover Cleveland, who was our president from '85 to '89, beat the incumbent Benjamin Harrison, to run our nation for another four years. I read in the newspaper that Sadie Boyd of Wyoming rode her horse 110 miles to Cheyenne, just to vote in the election. That would be like riding from here to Topeka. I wonder when the women of Kansas will get the right to vote.

November 24

The largest white gobbler from our flock was the centerpiece and main food for our Thanksgiving dinner today. On the table, there were mounds of fluffy mashed potatoes heaped high in the bowl with a pool of melted butter on top; corn smothered in fresh cream; sweet potato slices swimming in butter and sorghum molasses; layers of different kinds of pickles and preserves laid out on a serving tray; oven-warm biscuits, and sliced rye bread. There were so many bowls and platters of food that they couldn't all be set in the middle of the table at the same time! Mamma and I refilled bowls before they got halfway around our table of family and company. After all the time we spent making the pumpkin pies—scooping out the pumpkin seeds, peeling and cooking the vegetable's innards, mixing the custard and baking the pies, the thick slices overloaded with whipped cream were devoured in minutes. In some ways, fixing today's meal was no more work than usual for our large family, but being a holiday means you want the turkey browned just right and no lumps in the gravy. I'm a good cook, but I wonder if I could time everything just right like Mamma does. She said it just takes years of practice. On this day of counting blessings, I'm thankful I have Mamma to teach me.

December 10

The Assaria Ladies Sewing Society held a sale yesterday and made $100.35 for the new church organ fund.

Mamma came home with the news that Thomas Montgomery's 14-year-old son, who had been injured when thrown off a horse recently, died of lockjaw this week.

Crossing the river, she met a group of jackrabbit hunters. There have been several jackrabbit hunts in the area now that the ground is covered with snow. The rabbits are so numerous they are being sent to Denver, Chicago and St. Louis for their meat and hides.

December 19

Such a silent day and so somber. When I walked home from the Stenfors' farm, the fog enveloped the field in total silence, even though there were cows munching on the cornstalk stubble. Lining the edge of the road I traveled, the spent brown weeds were frosty frozen echoes of their former self. I pondered on the reasoning that everything that lives has to die. The Stenfors' six-week-old baby Lillie died yesterday. I brought over food for their noon meal, but it sits untouched. The silence in the house was as still as the fields I passed. Many young deaths have saddened our neighbors this year.

December 29

The pews of our church were full of beaming parents tonight for the Christmas Sunday School program. The littlest class always surprises you the most. Several children never took their eyes off their teacher, mimicking every word of the song a half second after she sang it. One girl knew the songs by heart and bellowed them out of her lungs in an off-pitch serenade of her own. Two boys wandered on and off the stage, not paying any mind to Pastor trying to motion them back up with the group.

At the end of the program, the teachers handed each of their pupils a gift from under the loaded Christmas tree as they marched out of the front pews. Many received miniature books, but members of Julia's class each got a glass Christmas ornament.

This has been a special Christmas for Julia. Peter thought she was old enough for a china doll this year. She is so careful with everything that I know it will always be cherished. I still have the doll that Papa gave me for Christmas when I was very small. Since our young family was struggling on the new homestead, Papa didn't have money like Peter does now, but the cloth-bodied doll with the wooden head carved by Papa will always be special to me.

Mabel, age 3 and Julia, age 7

1893

Chicago World's Fair

January 17

News about the Hawaiian Islands have been in the newspaper lately. Problems in their government and ours has caused the Queen of Hawaii to fall from her monarchy. I think the plan is to annex Hawaii to the United States eventually. I remember reading in school how these islands in the Pacific Ocean are always warm and the vegetation is green year round. American ships have sailed back and forth for years to harvest the whales that swim in their warm waters during the winter. These giant mammals provide the whalebone stays in our corsets and their blubber is melted down into oil for our lamps.

January 25

While trading at Assaria today in Olson & Linderholm's, a salesman was there demonstrating a phonograph playing music by means of electricity. The younger pupils from the grade school had been brought to the store for the demonstration.

Electricity has opened the door to so many new inventions in our world. The shopkeeper told me about Thomas Edison who is perfecting the first motion picture. Imagine seeing moving photos.

I'll be 20 years old in two days. I've seen and heard of so many new inventions while I've grown up. I wonder how the world will change in the next 20 or 40 years of my life. Some say that inventors are actually working on making these new moving pictures talk.

February 16

This week while we have a warm spell, we've been husking and shelling corn stored in the new granary last fall. It's one of those jobs you have to do now and then when the supply runs low. Shelled corn is fed to the animals as a supplement with their hay during the winter. After twisting the corn husks off, the dry shucks are thrown in the pig pen or chicken house for bedding. Years ago, instead of coal, we used to use the husks along with buffalo chips for fuel in our house stoves.

One winter project we've all helped on is tearing down the old granary. I've helped by pulling the square nails out the boards the boys have taken off the side walls. The nails will be hammered straight and used again if possible. The good wood will be reused for the new barn that will be raised this spring. Plans are to eventually tear down the little barn too.

One of the most solemn church services, besides funerals, is the Lent Day service. When we entered the church tonight, only half of the kerosene lanterns hanging from the ceiling were lit to give a subdued feeling to the congregation. After receiving communion, Pastor rubbed the sign of the cross on our foreheads with ashes to remind us of the death and sacrifices of Jesus. Communion will not be given again until Easter Sunday to celebrate the rising of Christ. We're all encouraged to give something up during the Lenten season as our own personal sacrifice. (I wonder if giving up thinking about boys qualifies?)

March 1

We spent the day at church, preparing food for the district conference that has been held the past two days. After we dried the dishes from the noon meal, we were able to slip into the back pews and listen to the rest of the afternoon speeches.

Willie was left in charge of Mabel so we didn't have to bring her along. Today he was sorting the best ears in the granary's corn crib for planting next month. The largest kernels shelled from the biggest ears will produce larger and stronger plants.

Mabel was playing in and out of the granary, sometimes stacking the ears Willie threw aside, or talking to the dog or cats.

Suddenly, with a thump, Willie was in the dark. Mischievous Mabel had shut the crib door and crawled up on an overturned bucket to turn the wooden block that holds the door closed. No amount of coaxing, begging or threatening from Willie would persuade Mabel to open the door. Alfred, who was cleaning out the chicken house nearby, finally heard Willie's yells and came to his rescue.

March 17

Although Irishmen were celebrating St. Patrick's Day with a parade in Chicago today, we were scooping paths to the outbuildings after being surprised by a late snow blizzard last night. At least the snow won't last on the ground, now that March breezes are warming the air this afternoon. Long dripping icicles draped down the side of the back porch, glistening in the sunlight until the weight of the ice made them crack and crash to the ground.

March 24

In today's newspaper, there was a full page article and drawing of the amusement ride that will be featured at the Chicago World's Fair. Four hundred men are working on it day and night to get it ready for the May 1st opening of the fair. Designed by W. G. Ferris, it looks like a giant bicycle wheel, standing 264 feet tall that will revolve between two towers. Fastened around the perimeter are 36 passenger coaches with upholstered seats that will carry 60 people each high into the air for a twenty-minute bird's eye view of the fair. Covered with 3,000 colored lights, I bet it will be a sight to see, day or night. It was stressed in the article that this structure has been engineered to withstand wind equal to a tornado blowing 100 miles an hour and is as safe as riding a train on the ground.

March 31

Alfred was confirmed today. Mamma has been worried that he would never finish since he was much older than the rest of the class. Visiting after church I heard that a telephone company has been organized in town. At first it will be used as a musical instrument entertainer. Singing into the transmitter at one house produces music on the other end of the wire at another home. George McPhail and John Olson plan to have a central office and be the musicians. Imagine having music in your home every evening. Life is so much more advanced in town than the prairie. I wonder when country life will catch up.

April 6

Raising of our new barn roof came to a quick halt as the men on top could see a big blaze northwest of the river. Neighbors scrambled off the building platforms and raced to the fire. Apparently the flames developed in the Cooper brothers' barn. Since the east wind was strong today, the fire spread across the grass, jumped the river and burned Sam Young's ice house and sheds. If the bridge being built east of Assaria would have been finished, the men could have gotten across the river and maybe stopped the fire. But unless someone catches the first flicker with a shovel or wet gunnysack to smother it, fire can spread very rapidly when the wind is working against you. At least neither house was lost. No more work was done on our barn today.

The new barn

April 28

Several news items in this week's paper were about the Chicago World's Fair. Opening a year late, the Columbian Exhibition, as it is officially called, evolves around the theme of the 400th anniversary of Columbus discovering the Americas, and is aimed to illustrate scientific advances in industry. Chicago was picked to host the fair because it is a major rail hub. People are expected to come from all over the world to see the exhibits.

Plaster used in the fair buildings came from Gypsum City's Ore Mill. The company will also have a display of their product at the fair. The mill ships out nearly 50 carloads of plaster a day.

Railroad tickets going to Chicago for the fair, good for the next six months, are on sale now at the depot. Minnie writes that for her September birthday, she is going to ride the train to Chicago to visit her sister Bessie, who works in that city, and explore the fair.

May 4

The men are still planting corn this week, so I am running the errands. I heard in town that J. B. Potter is making egg cases in Assaria. A cracker factory is said to be the next manufacturing venture to be coming into town. In the general store window were posters advertising the Ringling Brothers' World's Greatest Show that will be in Salina May 15th and the Cook & Whitby Colossal English Circus, Museum and Menagerie show on the 24th. The railroads have special rates going to Salina for the shows, but I doubt we'll go to either since we are busy with spring planting.

May 19

Immigrants heading back from the Cherokee Strip passed by here and camped near David Eagles across the river. We later found out that Eagles lost a pig and some corn was taken from his crib. Mr. Fairchild was robbed of four hams and canned fruit and Perills lost some dishes. Either these people were crooked or desperate to feed their families. Maybe they had high hopes to better themselves in a fresh start on new land. But after viewing the crowds already waiting for the opening of the Strip and the barren prairies of Oklahoma, they are trying to make it back to wherever home was before they left.

May 27

A bicycle store and repair shop has opened in Assaria. The newly formed bicycle club is practicing to get ready to ride to Chicago to the World's Fair. Jaunts are taking them all over the countryside on the best roads they can find.

Salemsborg will be starting the building of the their new church soon. Several carloads of lumber have arrived at the Assaria Depot.

Crawford & Breese Company of Salina is doing the building. The steeple, planned to be 156 feet tall on the white-framed church, will show up a long ways on the prairie.

June 15

Received a good rain today which we really needed for the corn and potatoes. Last week we had a dust storm that pitted the corn leaves and dried out the soil. The tender impatiens I mixed in Mamma's old flower bed look bruised, but the prairie perennials seem to thrive on bad weather. The rare pink yarrow I dug out of the pasture last summer is showing off its first round of flowers. Whenever I chance upon an unusual prairie flower, I try to transplant it around the house somewhere. Usually I have good luck, but certain plants seem to wither and die no matter how many times I've tried to transplant them. It is as if they prefer to live on the open prairie, taking their chances with moisture rather than being crowded into a flower bed, with plenty of water and attention.

August 5

Threshing machines devouring wheat stacks have made men hungry as they work to feed the smoke-belching machine. Us women have been working just as hard in the steaming kitchen this week. It has been hot and miserable lately.

When I had to go to the well for more water before the men came in at noon, I splashed my face and arms with water to cool myself down. It didn't matter that I got my dress wet, because the heat quickly dried the cotton material. My apron has been wet all afternoon though because I've wiped the sweat off my face with it. When it's below freezing next winter, I need to remember this week's temperatures.

One of the modern conveniences we've added to the kitchen is a sink and hand pump. But the cistern, beneath the back porch, where the water for the hand pump comes from, is now empty until we get a good rain to refill it, so all our water is being carried into the house again.

I hear bits and pieces of news as I serve the men at the dinner table. They are disheartened because wheat is down to 33 cents a bushel at Bridgeport and the Assaria elevator isn't buying at all. Hay is selling for $6 a ton. With a severe crop failure in some parts of the country you think prices would be higher.

August 10

Sultry steaming day for our annual church picnic. There was not a hint of breeze through the grove trees. Slices from the watermelons that had been chilled in the ice house were devoured with relish after the potluck meal. I drank so much lemonade that I feel like my lips are permanently puckered. My long-sleeved white dress was drenched with sweat and my bangs stuck to my forehead under my straw hat. Instead of playing the games planned, most opted to find a shady spot under the canopy of the trees and visit.

Rolling thunderclouds built up to the west as we rode along the sunflower-lined road on the way home. It started to sprinkle on our last mile. Tonight's shower cooled down the hot roof of the house. The upstairs rooms have been sweltering hot at night, so we've been sleeping on the south porch where at least we get some breeze.

September 21

The boys returned from the Cherokee Strip run full of stories. Willie, Swan and neighbor boy Per Sjogren ventured down to Arkansas City, Kansas, on the train to watch the Oklahoma land rush. At the sound of the gun and a bugle call, six million acres of prairie in Oklahoma were opened for settlement. Photographers from newspapers around the world posed ready to get the best shot of the start of the race. One ingenious group built a platform above the dirt cloud to get an overall shot of the crowd stampeding across the starting line. The dust rose above the roar as 100,000 men and women raced by foot, horses, new buggies, creaking old wagons pulled by oxen and even bicycles to stake their flags on the 40,000 claims available. The tangle and jumble of careening wagons and horses thinned as the crowd spread across the prairie. Because the Outlet was fifty-eight miles wide and over hundred miles long, most of the boomers raced a great distance.

Thousands more were there just to watch like the boys. The shopkeepers in the towns along the border did a booming business of their own before the race. People trailed in weeks ahead from all parts of the nation, waiting for the run. Most places ran out of food before opening day. Water was a premium with so many people and animals crowded in a small area that had been trampled to continuous dust. Disgusted people traveling back north who didn't get a claim, said the country was very dry. The land was suitable for grazing cattle, but not for farm land, they said.

Willie came back with a photo of Indians dressed up in their dress costumes. America's native people stood by and watched the range land they had roamed for thousands of years become dissected into crowded little farms in a matter of hours. Visions of ancient buffalo herds trailing for miles and miles over the endless prairie were cruelly over ridden in their minds by the sight of the white man seizing control of their once free land.

October 9

Bethany College played its very first football game Saturday. It is a new sport that is being played on the college campuses. Unfortunately, they lost 38 to 0 to Kansas Wesleyan College in Salina.

The men are finally sowing wheat this week. We've been stalling our wheat planting until we got some moisture. When the heavens finally let loose and rained a week and a half ago, we had to wait again for the fields to dry out enough to get in the fields. The subsoil moisture has been replenished so the wheat germination should be high.

The pumpkins and winter squash shells have hardened so we drove the wagon near the harvested pile in the garden, loaded up the heavy armloads and transported them to the cellar. I lost count of the number of trips up and down those steps. Us country girls definitely have muscles in our arms from all the heavy farm work we do.

October 15

The *Lindsborg News* reports that fire destroyed John Lamer's barn, five miles northeast of Lindsborg Friday night. Besides the contents of the building, he lost two horses and a mule. The paper didn't say how the blaze started.

Also mentioned in the paper was that a group of 100 people from the area traveled to the World's Fair this week. It is estimated that 27 million visitors will have viewed the exhibits by the time the fair closes at the end of the month.

Minnie's glowing report of the fair in her latest letter almost made me jealous. As souvenirs she brought home a charcoal portrait of herself and Bessie, and a tiny red glass mug with her name etched on it. She described the exhibits in the grand halls and listening to the people from all over the world as they exclaimed in their native language about the displays. Minnie said the ferris wheel, shining with thousands of lights in the festive night, effortlessly revolved on its axles so they viewed the tops of the buildings and the multitude of people that looked like ants below them.

November 15

I was glad for a reason to come in early from cornhusking this afternoon. Mamma wanted to go to the concert in the new Salemsborg Lutheran Church this evening. Tonight's program was for the dedication of the pews bought by the Young Men's Society. We didn't get to the first service in the new church that was on the 5th.

Mamma visited with old Salemsborg friends during the oyster supper they had in the basement after the program. Mrs. Samuel Johnson showed off her first grandchild, Theodore, born in February to her oldest son, Carl Oscar. Our family were members of the first dugout church Salemsborg built in '69 because it was the first church in our area. After more settlers homesteaded the county, the people in the eastern part of the Salemsborg congregation split away and organized the Assaria Church we attend now.

December 8

The bookstore in Lindsborg is advertising they have copies of the new Swedish books *Gud Hjalper* and *I Lifvets Vår*. I was thinking that one of these might make a good Christmas gift for someone in the family this year. The English titles *Heroes of the Dark Continent, The Wild West* and *Around the World* sound like books Willie and Alfred would like. I usually give handmade presents, but books are welcome gifts for the whole family.

December 18

Aunt Magda married Nels Johnson today. He has been her hired man since Uncle Erick, Mamma's brother, died from pneumonia five years ago. Mr. Johnson came to America in '86 and worked on Pete Olson's farm until his sister, Magda, needed help. Pete and Magda's parents, Olof and Kajsa Bryngelson, had been living with her and helping with the three young children since Erick died.

December 25

It is always a struggle to get up so early for *Julotta*, but to come out of church and see the sun rise on Christmas morning is worth it. Guiding us to the church in the dark this morning was the clear sound of instruments playing Christmas carols. Straining our ears, we could hear it a mile before we got to Assaria. Pulling into the churchyard and looking up, we spied the hunched shadows of the thirteen members of the Assaria Band serenading us from the church tower. Being 5 o'clock in the morning, their lips and fingers had to be numb from the piercing cold wind that blew through the tower, but their music sure warmed our hearts.

Standing: Christina, Alfred, Willie, Julia, Carrie and Alma.
Seated: Peter, Mabel and Kajsa.

1894

Willie's Adventure

January 26

I celebrated my 21st birthday a day early at Sewing Circle. The hostess served me the first piece of cake and coffee. I should say Women's Missionary Society since we decided today to reorganize and change the name. We will meet in homes two times a month to sew. Dues of 10 cents a meeting will be collected each month to help buy things needed in the church or missions around the world. If we don't get to the meetings, Mamma said we'll spend that time sewing at home for the cause.

February 16

Conditions were slick and fast for the sledding party on Uncle Andrew's pasture hill this afternoon. Peter and Uncle Andrew were waiting in their lumber wagons at school when the closing bell sounded to haul the merry bunch to the pasture. I mainly helped with refreshments, but Carrie and I got to go down the hill once together. We fell off, rolled down the slope and filled our bloomers full of snow. The bonfire felt good after the snow started to melt between my skin and my layers of clothing!

March 17

The wind blew so hard this afternoon that it was completely dark for 10 minutes. Coming home from town, we were all caught in the worst of it. Mamma wanted a family portrait taken, so we were in our best clothes, which had to be cleaned before we attend Palm Sunday service at church tomorrow. We just had a good rain last week, but the wind worked so hard at the wet topsoil it dried out and swirled in the air. A neighbor came by later reporting the wind had blown the roof off of Eberhardt's Lumber shed in town.

March 25

A prayer for Magnus Fager and his family was said in church this morning. He died at Uncle Frank and Aunt Emma's last week. Seems like the pioneers of the community are aging and passing on to their next journey.

Drove by the remains of Price Perrill's barn, house and outbuildings on 4th Street in Assaria that burned the other night. Mr. Perrill lost $5000 in property, his law books and one cow. He was able to save some household items. A tramp was later arrested for setting the fire.

Gathered eggs early this morning before church for the Easter egg offering. We are given new life since Christ died on the cross for us, so we give eggs, a symbol of a new life, to the church treasury on Easter.

A few dozen of yesterday's eggs were set back for this afternoon's Easter egg hunt for Julia, Mabel and our young cousins that joined them. After we hard boiled the eggs, we dyed the eggs in pickled beet juice for pink, onion skins for yellow and dandelion leaves for green. Carrie and I hid the eggs while the children waited inside. The dog found and ate the more obvious ones before the eggs were discovered by the children.

Yesterday's newspaper had an article about the Easter Monday egg rolling at the White House in Washington, D. C. that will be held tomorrow. No one is sure when this tradition started, but the 20-acre lawn is open to thousands of children, from dusk to dawn, to roll their eggs on the grassy slopes. After the children eat lunch, mainly hard-boiled eggs, the President holds a reception at two o'clock for all his visitors. When the day ends, the lawn is covered with broken egg shells of many colors.

April 10

The peach and early crabapple blossoms were black this morning from last night's frost. Mamma's mood is black too. She's sad, and being a mother, worried because Willie left this morning for California. He had talked about seeing the world for some time. Willie almost left last year, but he and Swan decided to see the Oklahoma Strip run last September, so he waited until now to leave. Being short of help in the fields now means I'll be helping more outside. Which is really fine with me, since I'd rather be outside working with the horses than being inside during spring cleaning. And at 10 and 6, Julia and Mabel are old enough to help Carrie and Mamma with household chores.

April 21

The newspaper reported a tornado passed through McPherson Tuesday night, destroying several buildings. Hopefully we'll hear more news about that cyclone soon.

The Assaria town council has voted to buy ladders and buckets for a fire department. With all the fires they have had in town, they need to be equipped for such emergencies.

Talking of fires, I had a close call when we were burning cornstalks this morning. We're clearing the fields to get ready to plant corn next week. I wasn't watching my business and my skirt brushed against the ignited stubble, causing it to catch on fire. Alfred tackled me and we rolled in the dirt to extinguish the flaming material. Luckily I didn't get burned. I shudder to think what would have happened if my petticoats had burst into flames too. I would have burned to death in the middle of the cornfield.

May 25

Since Bethany's commencement and Grand Concert are today, we decided to do our shopping in Lindsborg before the evening concert. Bethany's orchestra did a beautiful job playing selections from Haydn's *Creations*. Professor N. A. Krantz played an exceptional organ solo. He played at the Salemsborg Church last month when they dedicated their new pipe organ.

One of the main items on our shopping list today was glass canning jars. (Lindholm's in Assaria has fruit jars in their store, but Mamma thought we could get them cheaper in Lindsborg.) Each winter a few jars crack or break so we buy replacements. We usually can over 100 quarts of tomatoes alone, so we use hundreds of jars to preserve enough food for the whole year. Even though the cherries and plums are scarce this year we should have some fruit to put up. On the way home we each had a box of dozen jars on our laps, trying to cushion their rattling as we bounced home in the wagon. Mamma had thought to bring towels along to weave between the jars so they didn't touch each other.

May 30

The funeral was held yesterday for John O. Johnson, who had run the hardware store in Assaria for a while. He had been living with his parents two miles northwest of us. John was going home from Assaria with a dresser bureau in his wagon that had been shipped to him from Kansas City. His team spooked, throwing him from the wagon and breaking his neck. John and Christine, who is my age, were just married three weeks ago.

We walked the tracks to Bridgeport for the Memorial Day festival since it rained last night, and it was too muddy to go around with the buggy. The rain cut down on the attendance.

I know some people from Assaria were going to take the excursion train to Fort Riley for the festivities.

June 23

I read in the *Salina Sun's* Assaria column that last Monday lightning struck the house north of Mr. Herebners, passed down the flue, burst the stove pipe and scattered the stove around the room. Even though the accident filled the room with soot, there was no other damage to the house.

The newspaper also said the Topeka populist convention adopted women's suffrage. Susan B. Anthony put on a yellow badge, and whooped it up for the new faith. Mary Elizabeth Lease was quoted last year, "We should raise less corn and more hell." I know she meant the farmers, but I would like the chance to vote my opinion at the polls too.

July 2

The neighborhood is busy harvesting. Besides watching the weather during harvest, now we have to worry about the wheat after we've cut it. All seven wheat stacks on Nels Johnson's land east of Bridgeport were burned last night. The fire was supposedly started by tramps. He lost 1,500 bushels of wheat.

Julia and Mabel walked to Bridgeport to get last week's mail and found another letter waiting from Willie.

His first letters described the scenery along the train's route to California. The rolling tree-bare prairie in southern Kansas and the reverent mountain range in New Mexico turned into desert scenery in Arizona and California. He ended his train ride in Fresno, California. Standing on the platform gawking at the bustling town, his attention was drawn to a man in a buckboard yelling to the newly arrived crowd, "Can anyone here build a fence?" Willie got his first job.

Years working in our wheat fields prepared Willie for his next job, but on a much larger scale. He is spending the whole summer harvesting wheat on a 5,000 acre ranch in the San Joaquin Valley. It never rains there during the summer, so they can cut wheat every day without worrying about getting stuck in mud holes. Huge headers pulled by 48-horse teams, commanded by gees and haws, go out to the fields in the morning and never see the ranch buildings until the end of the day. Proving he could handle teams of horses was no challenge for him. Willie handled a team and scraper when he was a teenager and helped build the railroad grade that runs through our township.

Mamma was concerned when reading that the men had to lift sacks of threshed wheat that contained two and a quarter bushels of wheat each. At 135 pounds a sack a person would have to lift them just right not to injure their backs. Wagons are strung together with three teams of horses hitched to the front to haul the wheat to the rail station. He thought part of the harvest was shipped to the coast where ships would cargo it to other countries.

Our brother says he wishes he could see one of his sisters coming over the hill with a pitcher of fresh lemonade and a basket of home baked cookies.

July 7

The chore of milking the cow did not deter my mind from wandering as I watched the dust flecks dancing in the sunbeam that shone through the crack in the barn door. A devastating hailstorm hit Brookville the night we had rain. The ice stones broke 70 windows out of the school, killed chickens, perforated tin roofs and severely damaged the corn and fruit trees. What would our place look like this evening if we had had that hail too?

August 15

Carl August Nathanial Olson increased neighbors Pete and Hannah Olson's family today. Their oldest daughter Alma, sent Emma, Joe, Hilda and Gottfrid to our house to give their mother some peace and quiet. Emma is Julia's age and Hilda is Mabel's best friend, so the six of them had a good time together. Most of their time was spent outdoors playing under the shade tree within sight of the kitchen window. The boys took command of the rope swing for a while, glad to get away from their chores at home for a few hours. The four little barefoot girls set up housekeeping, drawing the boundaries of the house with a stick in the dirt. You could hear them tattle when one forgot to use the 'door' and walked through the 'wall' instead. Mabel sneaked into the kitchen to steal some flour for their mud pies. She thought if they mixed flour and water into a paste they could frost their brown mud pies with white icing.

August 19

This morning we attended the Sunday services at Bethany Church for their 25th anniversary celebration. Pastor Olof Olsson, who founded the church in 1869, traveled from Illinois for the occasion. Mamma said that my grandparents *Farfar* and *Farmor* were in his first congregation.

We noticed several improvements in Lindsborg since we were last there in May. New brick walks replaced the board walks on the west side of Main Street. The new engine house at the mill is running. Peter commented that the mill's production is up to 150 barrels of flour a day.

September 13

This afternoon we attended the AOUW Lodge picnic at David Eagles grove, east of town. Assaria won the baseball game against Salina. The children tumbled in a pile at the end of the tug of war. I rode in Alfred's wheel barrel for that race because he was too shy to ask anyone but his sister. Besides, I didn't have a beau to ask me.

Since we had a fine-misting rain early last week, it softened up the soil so we got the rye planted. Most farmers have already cut up the corn for fodder since it dried up by the end of August this year. This is probably the last social get-together for the community until after the field work is done.

October 1

Mabel's first day of school. The new teacher is going to have his hands full since she can be so rambunctious. Julia came home embarrassed because Mabel raised her hand for every question today, even though she didn't know the answers. Those two are opposites in nature.

October 4

Aunt Marie and Millie visited us while Uncle Andrew went to the Populist meeting at Star School tonight with Peter and Albert. They said there were forty present, six being Republicans and no women, even though they said we ladies were welcome. I'd rather visit at home than listen to the men argue politics.

They brought news that Dr. Crawford is leaving his Assaria practice. Peter also said that the little fires we saw recently at night to the west have been wheat stacks that someone is setting on fire around Bridgeport again.

November 4

It was still warm enough to stand outside after church to visit this morning. I noticed some of Assaria's businessmen had given hard stares at a certain group of young men that had acted like angels in their pews this morning. Somebody piled boxes in front of the stores downtown as a Halloween prank Wednesday night. Serious news was that Lamer and Wells lost 20 head of cattle to thieves last weekend.

November 29

We caught a ride at Bridgeport on the south-bound train to attend the annual Thanksgiving Concert in Lindsborg tonight. Trains ran from Salina and McPherson for it. After finishing the harvests, we were ready to give thanks with song.

December 25

Christmas didn't seem right with Willie missing from our family circle around the Christmas tree last night. Three weeks ago, we sent him a package of presents and a carefully wrapped tin of Christmas cookies, but we have no idea if he received it. I put in a copy of Mark Twain's new book, *The Tragedy of Pudd'nhead Wilson*. We had a very limited supply of books in our school library when we were in school, but I remember Willie was fascinated with Twain's books on Tom Sawyer and Huckleberry Finn.

Here, we have snow covering our brown pastures and he last wrote that the California hills, which turn brown from May to December from lack of rain, now have a hint of green because they have started their rainy season. It sounds like their season of greenery is opposite of ours.

Ling Auditorium on the Bethany College campus

1895

Bethany's Auditorium

January 20

What's the world coming to these days? Thieves broke into the Bridgeport Post Office and stole stamps last night. These bad characters also stole clothing and canned goods from another store. Last week the safe was blown up at the Lindsborg Mill. The crime rate is rising in our area towns.

January 27

My 22nd birthday. Still no prospects of marriage in the near future. I believe it is time I think about how to support myself. Granted I'm needed and welcome on the farm, but I'd like to be on my own someday. Career choices for unmarried women are teacher, hired household help or seamstress. I don't have enough schooling to become a teacher and I'd rather not hire out to do laundry and cooking for some old widower's family. Good positions like the one Minnie has in Kansas City would require me to leave the area, and I don't want to move if possible.

When our township was just getting settled, women in the area did their own sewing because they couldn't afford anything else. Now with the large families prospering on the established farms, maybe I could help sew their family's clothing. Most families average six to ten children around here. Even though the younger children get the hand-me-down clothing from the older ones, the old clothes may need to be altered and new clothes made when they wear out. It would be a respectable employment for a young woman and I believe Mamma would agree to it.

February 6

Today was a day they call not fit for man nor beast. I'd say by the velocity of the wind and the height of the drifts, this is the biggest blizzard we've had so far this year. It will take awhile to dig out of this one.

This morning Julia and Mabel raced downstairs and dressed in front of the kitchen stove because it felt like the freezing wind was coming right through the bedroom walls. Today they didn't complain about their itchy long underwear.

February 26

It was warm enough today that it sprinkled this afternoon as Peter and Alfred made their way home from Assaria. First time any of us has gone into town since the blizzard.

Mamma always asks what's new in town. I believe it's a habit from years ago when it would be months between trips off the homestead for her. Peter is always ready with the news.

Olof Melander is tearing down McPhail's old elevator in Assaria. Mrs. Fred Stevens will be starting a vocal class in Bridgeport. Mr. Ekstrand is moving his Bridgeport drugstore to Assaria and J. B. Smith is moving his store and post office from Bridgeport to Assaria.

The AOUW Lodge is raising money for a town hall in Assaria. So far the organization has raised $1,000, but $1,000 more is needed. The plan is a two-story building, the hall above and two stores on the main floor.

March 16

The temperature dropped drastically yesterday. These cold waves are very hard on the cattle. We moved two newborn calves into the barn because they were shivering so bad. I rubbed them down with gunny sacks to get their circulation going. One little calf's nose was blue until I brought him in and warmed him up. The mamma cows don't like to be separated from their babies, but I'll unite them later in the barn box stalls. The calves need their mother's first milk as soon as possible, but they need to be able to stand up first.

March 25

We welcomed a new little cousin into the family today as Arthur Nathanial was born to Aunt Magda and Nels. Magda's older children,

Emelia, Hulda and Martin are aged between Julia and Mabel, so Arthur will be the baby of our family. Born two days later, he would have arrived on Mabel's seventh birthday.

April 1

Stepping out the back door in the early dawn to go to the outhouse, I nearly slipped and fell. Mother Nature played a dirty April Fool's trick on us today coating the ground and trees with a thick layer of ice. The freezing rain turned to snow by noon. The first daffodils with their heads nodding from the weight of the ice looked confused, as if to say "Did we come up too soon?" I hope the weather clears for the people going to the *Messiah* concert Wednesday.

April 5

A caravan of Liberty young people converged on the masquerade ball in Bridgeport tonight. Everyone goes to events as a group usually, picking neighbors up along the way. Carrie made sure she rode in Per Sjogren's buggy. I believe there is a match in the air.

I've had a few dates, but nothing serious that would make my heart flutter and put a spark in my eyes like the way Carrie is acting. All the area farm boys seem like brothers to me since we grew up together. I've daydreamed about the handsome man that will carry me off into the sunset someday. Where is he?

April 13

Clouds of soft pink and white petals scented the air among the orchard trees as I left the farm for town. I hope we have a good crop this year. Last season's late freeze left me hungry for cherries all year. Arbor Day prompted Molander's and Lundal's to line their properties with fruit trees in Assaria. Seventy spindly trees planted along their street will put on a showy display in a few years as the trees mature.

One of the hats in Miss Olson's hat display in Lindholm's store reminded me of apple blossoms. A sprig of pink silk flowers and emerald green ribbon, the color of new leaves, decorated the straw summer bonnet. With my sewing money, I could afford to buy a new spring hat.

April 19

Spring cleaning was extra rigorous this week since Mamma hosted the Women's Missionary Society meeting today. Eleven women, mostly from our township, plus a surrey full from town graced our parlor. Elsa Person (she remarried again after her second husband Olaf Hessler died) brought along her four-year-old daughter Louisa to play with Mabel. Julia went home with Millie after the meeting to spend the night with our cousin.

Peter and Alfred didn't even come in for afternoon coffee, preferring to wait until the last woman had left the homestead to come inside and eat the leftovers. Mamma was very particular about the coffee (two raw eggs to clarify the brew) and food we served for refreshments. Only the best-looking *spritz* cookies were served. The pan that got overly brown in the oven was delegated for family only, which was okay with us. One of the women asked for my White Delicate Cake recipe because it was so good. I pulled out the old ledger book that I've written recipes in and made her a copy. (The secret to this light cake is the seven egg whites and a teaspoon of lemon extract.)

May 30

Today's steady downpour has kept us inside and away from Memorial Day services. Rain seems to be the trend on this holiday. I guess it goes with the somber thought of remembering our dead. Mamma was upset that she hadn't gotten to Assaria to decorate her parent's graves before the rains. The peony flowers, which have been beautiful this week, are dropping their petals in the soaking rain. By the time the roads are dry enough to get to the Assaria cemetery, most of the peonies will be past. Mamma lamented she should have done it yesterday. Tomorrow I'll trudge up to Uncle Andrew's hill to put flowers on Papa's grave.

June 10

Rain flowed down the gutters as I reread Willie's latest letter and wondered what news of home to write back to him.

Willie started working in a vineyard in the valley after the wheat harvest was done. He spent the winter and early spring pruning the grapevines back to a main stalk while they were dormant. Now the vines have stretched to their limit, their energy flowing to the flowers that are turning into tiny grapes. Willie says the grapes grown for wine are more like the eating grapes we grow, not like the wild ones we pick for juice and jelly. During the summer months, the crew will be hoeing and tending the acres of trellised vines.

I can't think of much news to write to Willie. The wheat fields are very thin, and I predict it will be a poor quality crop. Peter says the oats will produce an adequate crop though.

As far as doing something besides farm and garden work, we're learning the game of croquet, which is now popular around here. Someone was saying that baseball is considered old-fashioned now, but I don't think that will cause the baseball teams around here to switch from bats to mallets.

July 7

The flash of lightning is adding to the light in the parlor as I write tonight, but the rumble of thunder is breaking my concentration.

News in the paper this week says that the telephone lines are up in Lindsborg and going on to McPherson. Lindsborg residents can talk to Gypsum and Brookville. Gypsum was mentioned again since thieves blew open the safe at the Gypsum City Roller Mills this last week to get $25.

July 8

The farmers and townspeople have been put to the test again by flood water from our last heavy rains. Creek water crept up the alley last night. We walked the tracks west this morning, and sure enough, Bridgeport is under deep water again.

July 26

Even though school is out, Bethany College is buzzing with carpenters this summer. Through persistence and amid criticism, Dr. Swensson has pursued his dream of building a grand concert hall on campus. He had been warned that it could cause financial ruin to the college, but he firmly believes it will help the college grow instead. Railroad carloads of donated lumber are being crafted to create Ling Auditorium. Their deadline is October 3 because they have already announced the Grand Concert for its dedication.

September 21

Willie's letter from me will be a blotted ink stain by the time I'm done writing. It has been 105 degrees all week. I can't remember a time in September that has been this hot for so long. Willie wrote describing the cool nights in the valley now that they are harvesting the grape clusters to be crushed. I wish he could send some cool weather to Kansas in his envelope.

I wrote back that the telephone lines are working in Assaria now, connecting the town to Salina, Brookville, Gypsum and Bavaria. Next month Assaria will be connected with Lindsborg and McPherson too. It cost $100 to join the telephone company and get an instrument. Telephone call bells are going to be installed at J.H. Johnson's house, Lindholm's store and the hardware store.

October 4

It was a gorgeous Indian summer day for the opening of Ling Auditorium. Bethany, Salemsborg and Fremont bands marched in the parade to commence the dedication.

Men's, women's and children's choruses of 300 voices swelled in the auditorium for the opening of the Forefathers Day Celebration. I recognized people from Assaria mixed in the choirs. An orchestra and military band of 125 accompanied the singing. I believe every seat in the round auditorium that holds 4,000 people was filled. His Majesty, King Oscar II of Sweden-Norway donated the Swedish flag and President Cleveland sent the American flag. Our Kansas Governor Morrill spoke at the morning program and Senator John Ingalls gave the afternoon address. We didn't stay for the evening program. Tomorrow's three programs will pay tribute in a Patriotic Festival to America's independence in 1776, Kansas statehood in 1861 and the era of Ling Auditorium in 1895. If the weather holds I hope to go to the afternoon program on the Bridgeport train.

October 28

Today was my first day at the dress cutting school being taught in Assaria by Lulu Mysten of Gypsum. I'm a good seamstress, but I know I'll gain knowledge and confidence sewing for others by learning more about patterns and design. It's one thing to cut down a dress to fit a child, but quite another to fit a man's suit properly. Patterns have to be laid a certain way for the grain of material and to match lines. I just cringe now when I see an ill-fitted suit or a dress where the plaids don't match.

November 1

The roads are bad from yesterday's rain, so I stayed in Assaria with friends last night instead of going home after school. Being in Assaria on Halloween night wasn't so spooky this year because a marshal was posted on every street corner to squash any mischief.

November 30

I read the first automobile race was held Thursday between Chicago and Waukengan, Illinois. The 52-mile race was won by Charles Duryea who invented the first horseless buggy two years ago. I've seen pictures of one, but as of yet haven't seen this kind of transportation on Liberty Township roads. Is it possible that one day we'll be going to town in an automobile instead of by horse and buggy?

December 20

Perry Rittgers' home, a half mile north of us, was bulging with the young people of Liberty tonight. The Rittgers gave a wonderful Christmas party with caroling and games, like spin the bottle. I helped make popcorn balls, while the men buttered their hands to pull taffy. Since the Rittgers are English, they have different holiday traditions and food than us Swedes. The Swedish custard dessert *ostkaka* wasn't on their menu tonight.

December 31

I think half our neighborhood converged on Ling Auditorium this evening with all of Assaria, Bridgeport and Lindsborg. The Luther League sponsored a *lutfisk* supper to celebrate New Year's Eve. I can't believe how much of that smelly fish they had to soak, wash and cook for the hundreds of people they served. Several area bands played, along with the audience singing all the favorite Christmas carols, both English and Swedish.

As I look back on the year, I feel I have grown more towards being a responsible adult. I've expanded my horizons beyond the farm boundaries by doing some sewing for other people. I'm proud of my work and confident I can make a living at it.

Wedding picture of Per and Carrie Sjogren

1896

Carrie's Wedding

January 27

My 23rd birthday. Looks like I'll be the old maid left at home yet. Carrie and Per Sjogren are going to marry this fall.

Some of the items we've been making for my trousseau may go into Carrie's instead if we don't get hers finished in time. Since she's just eighteen, she doesn't have enough quilts tops stitched or linens embroidered yet. She and I have started looking at dress designs in *Harper's Magazine* and *Ladies Home Journal* to get ideas for her wedding gown. Sears and Roebuck has come out with a bigger catalog this year that features all kinds of merchandise, from buggies to clothing. I noticed that white is becoming a popular color for the bride's dress instead of black or gray. I'm glad I took the class last fall because I want to design the perfect dress for Carrie. Since completing the course, I have been collecting dress designs and patterns from the newspapers and magazines. Sometimes I sketch a design that pops up in my head. I need ideas to show my customers.

February 21

Today we hosted Women's Missionary Society at our house. Mamma likes to get the meeting in our neighborhood once a year so our neighbors can be a part of the group. While we sewed, Carrie told us her plans for next fall. Per is buying his father's land a half mile south of us to farm. After Nels Sjogren helps with his son's fall harvest, he plans to move to Lindsborg.

March 26

I delivered eggs to Assaria today so I could buy material for my latest project. Usually the wife of the family picks out the material, but Mrs. Mattson asked me to do it the next time I was in town. She recently delivered her ninth child and has her hands full right now. A bolt of white shirt material for the six boys was easy to pick out, but I looked through the selection more carefully for the girls' dresses. You can always tell who are sisters in a crowd because their dresses are all made from the same material. I wanted to find a colorful bolt of print that complemented Selma and Hilma Mattson, but different from what the other neighbor girls might have. I bought extra to make the new baby Lillie a little dress too.

While shopping, I heard that John Larson's house in town almost burned down earlier this month, when a blanket left by the stove apparently started the fire. Fortunately a group of neighbors got the blaze out. Assaria is considering buying a fire engine so the entire town doesn't get wiped out someday.

It sounds like that almost happened in Gypsum Tuesday noon. The post office and six buildings burned down. The fire started in the bakery, then spread both directions to the meat market, barber shop, grocery store and jewelry store.

April 3

We rode the train from Bridgeport to Lindsborg to hear the Good Friday performance of the *Messiah*. The 138 voices in the *Messiah* choir gave the 1,000 crowded into the chapel an excellent program. As is tradition, we stood for the "Hallelujah" chorus. Before the concert we toured the art department's exhibit in the auditorium. Three altar pieces, entitled *There Were Shepherds, Christ in Gethsemane* and *He Shall Feed His Flock* were the center of attention. I don't know what churches in the area these paintings will be hanging in eventually, but they will cherished forever.

May 1

Last week's soaking rain had made the wheat look so good, but one day of bad weather changed that. Yesterday morning, frost covered the ground. Later in the day wind and dust blew until we were afraid the wheat was going to be blown out of the ground. I'm sure the crop was damaged by wind.

May 16

Today we mourn the tragic death of a neighbor boy. Ralph Young, who lived west of Robinson's, was fishing on the river and the bank gave way above him. Big clods fell on his head and broke his neck. Mamma always warns us to respect the river when we go down to hunt or fish. The river may look calm, but the water and its banks can be unpredictable.

June 9

Our township was pounded by 4 inches of hard rain this week. Storms in western Kansas pushed the Smoky Hill River to its limit before it came through our drenched area. Standing on the train tracks there is water as far as the eye can see. This time water flooded past the barn and threatened to seep into the well.

The old sod dugout that Mamma and Papa first lived in collapsed from the heavy rains and flood. Somewhere under the pile of mud are some childhood marbles. When we were little, Willie and I would play marbles in the old house. He would aim for a certain knot hole in the wooden floor. I'd get so upset with him when Willie's shot was a bull's eye because it meant we lost another marble. "Don't cry, Alma," he'd say to me. "Someday there will be lots of little marbles." When I write to Willie about the flood, I'll remind him he still owes me some marbles.

The bridge by Mr. Lapsley's house and the other small creek bridges around Liberty were all washed out by the rains.

Hiram Godley, who farms on the river, said the flood came up so fast that the family barely got upstairs before two feet of water rushed into their house. Furniture floated in the rooms until the water flowed back out an hour later. The milk, butter and fruit cans in his spring house disappeared down the river.

We weren't the only areas with problems. Windstorms and floods in Iowa, Illinois and Michigan killed 100 people last week.

July 4

Rain killed our chance to take the buggy to Lindsborg for the celebration, so we walked the tracks and took the train instead. The parade went on as scheduled, but the bicycles were omitted because of the muddy streets. The trains brought in large crowds for the day including several carloads from McPherson. This afternoon a crowd of 2,500 filled the auditorium to hear the Honorable J. R. Burton speak. Some say this eloquent speaker is headed for the U.S. Senate someday. The three-manual pipe organ (meaning three banks of keys) installed this summer was used for the first time today. The newspaper touted it as the finest organ in the West (expect for Denver and Salt Lake), at the cost of $5,000. Since the train didn't depart until after all the activities, we went back for the evening performance of music in the auditorium. Climatic fireworks in the hot summer night ended the festive day.

The glow of the moonbeam-lit tracks lit our path home from the Bridgeport Depot. Each of us recounted favorite parts of our day or news we heard while in town. Mamma said that Minnie Danielson, who lives near Lindsborg, was milking her cow in the pasture earlier this week when a bolt of lightning struck the cow, killing it and knocking Minnie unconscious. Mamma said Dr. Berquist restored the girl, and she will be fine. That's a story to add to both Willie's and Minnie Granquist's next letter.

July 15

Just sprinkled enough this morning to settle the dust so we didn't miss the Sunday school picnic at church today.

On the way to Assaria, we dropped off a half-gallon jar of milk for Mr. Lapsley since he's been feeling a little under the weather. With no cow of his own, he relishes a container of milk whenever a neighbor offers it to him.

August 19

It has been too dry for us to hitch up the team to plow this month, so we welcomed the rain this evening. It's is too late to help the stunted corn though.

We'll finish digging the rest of the potatoes and plant the late garden this week. I've already cleaned out old plants and vines that are done for the season, and have been waiting for a rain to soften the earth. Fall planted lettuce, spinach and radishes are usually big enough by the end of September to savor a taste of fresh vegetables again before frost hits. The seeds germinate and grow fast in the summer-heated soil, but don't go to seed since September evenings cool down the garden.

Fall grown turnips are harvested in October, topped and stored in the cellar for winter use. If some of the tubers get too big, or don't get dug before a hard frost, they are woody and bitter tasting to us, but the pigs enjoy them.

September 2

Listening to Carrie and Per repeat the wedding vows in our parlor made Mamma misty-eyed and Peter proud, since he helped raise her from a baby. Carrie looked radiant in her gown and veil. The crystal-beaded medallion we fastened to the cloud of veil illuminated her radiant face. Hours of hand stitching were required to attach the delicate lace to the white satin on the bodice of her dress. We worked on the dress in the cool early hours of the morning this summer so we didn't stain the dress with our afternoon sweat. Even though she will live nearby, this is the last project that we will work so closely on together.

Christina spent the week helping with everything from cleaning house to preparing food for the wedding dinner. Our aunts served the meal so Mamma could play the mother of the bride and remember the joy in the parlor, not the work in the kitchen.

Another sibling has left home.

September 14

The echoes of the bell ringing for the first day of school followed me up the hill as I drove north to Robinson's house. Mrs. Robinson has hired me to make winter clothing for her and Mr. Robinson. I'm sure they have had clothing made in Salina since their daughter Laura is married to a prominent judge, but I think she is helping me get my name established as a seamstress for hire in Liberty Township. I'll enjoy my work and visit with them.

October 6

Mr. Enander, editor of *Swedish-American* of Chicago spoke at Ben Hessler's grove today on sound money, true Republicanism and patriotism. It was a fine address in favor of William McKinley. You can tell it is a presidential election year by all the campaigning going on. This area has been especially informed on politics this round because Dr. Swensson of Bethany College was a delegate to the

Republican National Convention in St. Louis, where McKinley was nominated to run against William J. Bryan.

November 4

Along with the good news from Bridgeport that McKinley won in yesterday's presidential race came bad news about Willie. Mamma received a brief letter from a hospital in California where Willie is confined while he recovers from malaria. We pray that his health will return soon so he can travel home. Too bad he couldn't have been home for his sister's wedding. Carrie sent a copy of their wedding portrait to him last month, but the letter didn't say if he had received the picture.

November 26

All the men who have spent the last few weeks snapping corn congregated around the school stove while we set up the food on the long plank tables for our Thanksgiving dinner. The whole room gets rearranged when a big group moves in. Desks pushed aside, tables and chairs set up, scampering children underfoot everywhere. Bitter cold winds this morning kept a few families home from the far corners of our school district. It has become the tradition to have a group Thanksgiving dinner in the schools. The people planning the dinner at the Assaria school were counting on over a hundred people. They have service at the church first, while at Star School we had a program after our meal.

December 5

It has been a hard year, being a poor harvest and low market prices, but I have my seamstress earnings to spend this year for gifts. This morning I pondered over the trinkets Olof Carlson had displayed in his Assaria store for Christmas presents. Most families have paid me for my work by putting the eggs and butter they've sold to the store in my name for credit. Part of Mrs. Robinson's cash from her job went for a yardage of blue velvet for a new dress for me. The rest will be used for my Christmas church offering. I try to give the church four dollars a year.

1897

Mr. Lapsley's Heart

January 27

Our whole family is back under the same roof today. Christina is home this week to visit since Willie has returned from California. Even though he is still thin and weak from the malaria, being home to good Swedish cooking has done wonders for him since cousin Gus Neberg brought him home by train a few days ago. Willie is anxious to get back to farming here in Liberty Township after he recovers.

Willie's luggage concealed gifts for all of us. The biggest presents he hauled home were two huge conch shells for Julia and Mabel. The rough outside of the tan horn-shaped shell was a complete contrast to the light pink smooth insides. We all experienced the roaring ocean when Willie held the shells to our ears and described the rolling waves sliding in and out on the sandy beaches of the sea.

With a big grin on his face, Willie handed me a bag of marbles! He had forgotten that long ago promise until I mentioned it in my letter. He said my description of everyday events in the neighborhood helped him on lonely nights in a strange state where the scenery and climate were so different from home.

Carrie came over for coffee today for my 24th birthday and to hear of our brother's adventures. She surprised us with the news that she is expecting a baby next summer. I'm going to be an aunt! Christina was happy for Carrie, but I think a little sad since she and Swan have been married almost eight years without the chance of a family.

February 5

The Lindsborg newspaper mentioned that *Messiah* practice is starting soon. The performances will be in the auditorium this year where they will be able to seat 4,000 at each performance. I would love to sing in the *Messiah* some year, but with seven inches of snow on the level this week and bad weather half the time, how could I get to practice every Sunday afternoon and Tuesday evening for ten weeks?

March 20

Peter mentioned at supper tonight that John P. Olson and Olson Isaacson have a patent pending for a self-feeding threshing machine. He saw them working on it last summer and thinks their invention has a chance at the patent being granted.

A rumor around the checker board game in the Assaria general store was that the town hall will be built this spring on the vacant lot in the middle of the city. Assaria is big enough that a building could be used for everything from a court of law to dances and meetings.

April 1

Afternoon sprinkles chased me out to the clothes line to rescue the new fabric that I had washed to preshrink, but pelts of tiny sharp hail sent me scurrying back into the shelter of the porch. I hope the material isn't ruined. Through the pouring rain I could make out Peter standing in the barn door and Alfred in the granary, waiting for the storm to let up before bolting for the house for afternoon coffee. When the wind came up, we all retreated to the safety of our individual shelters. At least the rain will do the wheat some good, and it is still too small to be hurt by the hail.

Jobs with neighbors this spring have made it easy for me to work at home on our treadle sewing machine. After discussing what fabric and pattern to use for the new outfit, I take measurements and start on the project. Sometimes it's a very simple job of cutting down a mother's old dress to fit a youngster or two. If a formal or wedding dress is needed, I sketch my ideas so the customer can visualize the finished outfit. And I urge them to let me make a muslin pattern using the person's measurements first to make sure of the fit before cutting up expensive silk. Getting clothes to fit all sizes of bodies can be a challenge. I try to politely stress patterns and types of fabric to

INFORMATION!

About the "MESSIAH" at Bethany College at Linds-borg, Kansas, April 16th, 1897.

SPECIAL TRAINS.

Will leave Great Bend, Hoisington, Hutchinson and intermediate points from the west and Osage City, Council Grove, Herington, Hope and intermediate points from the east in time to reach Linds-borg at 6:45. The Afternoon Concert will be abbreviated some and rendered between 7:00 and 8:00 o'clock.

To those who attend the "MESSIAH" the Admission will be

ONLY 25 CENTS.

At 8:00 o'clock there will be a recess of 30 minutes for lunch in the beautiful and commodious DINING HALL of the College. Charges: Coffee, Sandwiches, &c., 5 cents each.

THE MESSIAH CONCERT

Will begin at 8:40, the same as last year. The Chorus and Orchestra are larger than last year. In addition we have the large New Three Manual Pipe Organ, and Miss Ernestine Cotton among the Soloists. Prof. Sigfrid Laurin is the Conductor; Prof. Franz Zedeler, the leader of the Orchestra; Prof. Samuel Thorstenberg, the Organist *Admission 50 cts.* The "MESSIAH" is the greatest Oratorio ever composed. It is immortal. It never grows old. Every one should hear it as often as possible.

EVERY VISITOR SHOULD ATTEND BOTH CONCERTS.

At the close of the Messiah Concert, refreshments will be served in the Dining Hall. Coffee, Sandwiches, &c., 5 cents. Ice Cream and Cake 10 cents.

A hearty welcome to all lovers of Music and of Education.

Direct all Communications to

CARL SWENSSON,

President of Bethany College, Lindsborg, Kansas.

79

minimize large busts and hips. It's hard to swallow my thoughts when a women picks out a color of fabric that doesn't suit her complexion or hair color. My job is to please the customer, but if the dress looks dreadful on the woman, my sewing reputation can be hurt.

April 3

Found out we were lucky with this last storm on the farm. It blew the roof off of Olof Peterson's barn and leveled several outbuildings in Bridgeport.

April 16

Each homestead we passed as we traveled to Lindsborg had a burst of color somewhere on the farm. The fruit trees look like they would explode if one more blossom pops out.

We have been to a few performances in Ling Auditorium, but the excitement of the *Messiah* being performed for the first time here today gave a shiver of anticipation to the waiting crowd. The chorus and orchestra had increased in size because of the additional space, and the sound magnified inside the round interior. Special trains came from as far away as Great Bend, Osage City and points in between. I saved my ticket stub since it was the first performance in Ling Auditorium.

May 3

Since the Lamkins sold their farm to the west of us a few years ago, it's had different families renting the farmstead, mostly English people. Now we have Swedish neighbors again, actually from our church. Peter Oborg and his wife Gunilla, who is a few years younger than me, have moved in this week. They are poor farmers without much to their name yet, but they've just been married three years.

They have two little boys, Olof, about two years old, and Luther, who is one.

They will be isolated down on the river by themselves with no road going by their farm. To get to their 100 acres, they must take the dirt track going west at the school house corner, between us and Olson's, cross the creek, follow the river back south and cross under the railroad track. The buildings are set up on the highest part of the land, so I don't think it has ever flooded, but they sure have a bird's eye view when it happens and will find out they won't be able to get out.

May 26

I hope the rain we received today helps the crops. The corn is looking promising, but the upland wheat has been suffering. The tops of the potatoes have recovered from late frost. For all the blooms on the fruit trees last month, we were planning on a bumper crop for the cellar, but fruit is only sparsely scattered on trees. The late frost shriveled the peony buds too so I won't have any peony blossoms this year.

Swan, Anna and Christina Nelson

June 1

Christina and Swan have adopted three-year-old Anna Forsberg. Her family came from Sweden four years ago and farmed north of Hallville. After the girl's mother died in April, her father longed to return to Sweden. He found a home for Anna and work for his older children, and left. Christina will make sure Anna keeps in contact with her siblings. The little girl will have a good life in Christina's home.

June 19

News of the devastating fire on Ellis Island last Tuesday night was on the front page of the newspaper today. The huge three-story main building caught fire during the night and spread to the other buildings on the island. The wooden structures couldn't be saved because the channel around the island was too shallow for the fire-fighting tugs to get close enough to spray the buildings. Eye witnesses reported it looked like the entire island was ablaze. By some miracle, no lives were lost. All the personnel and immigrants in the infirmary escaped to boats, but most of the records dating back to 1855 were destroyed. Speculation was that when the immigrant station is rebuilt, it will be made of brick instead of pine.

June 25

My heart almost stopped when I heard the girls screaming above the rumble of the approaching train. I could just imagine one of them having their foot stuck between the railroad ties on the track. Racing outside, I found another situation instead. Mabel and Julia had been picking currants along the railroad right-a-way. When they heard the chugging engine, they climbed over the fence between the tracks and our field. Mabel's skirt caught on the fence post and she flipped upside down. The grinning engineer waved and tooted his horn as Mabel hung there showing her blommered rear end to the passing passenger train.

July 2

We've sweltered in 100 degree temperature every day this last week. The threshing machines are busy, so we celebrated Julia's thirteenth birthday at noon with a table full of threshers. It was so hot in the house the frosting almost melted off the cake before dinner.

The men report the wheat is threshing good in this hot weather and to expect a good overall yield.

John Anderson said this is the best wheat he's ever had—20 bushels to the acre on his upland ground and 30 bushels on bottom land.

I know the wheat is good this year but the growing corn looks sickly. My garden has not yielded well. We'll only get half a crop of potatoes, stunted onions and no headed cabbage because of the heat.

July 17

After writing the date in my diary, I realize it was twenty years ago today that Papa was killed by lightning. Papa and Mabry, our hired man, had been working in a field northeast of here, got caught in a storm and were walking home. It happened when Papa's parents farmed caddy-corner from the school house. I remember *Farmor* screaming as she ran through the garden to tell Mamma after they had been found. Even though I was only four years old when it happened, I remember some details. The smell of burnt flesh and the sight of charred bodies can never be erased from a child's mind. Because the storm had flooded the river and we couldn't get to the Assaria cemetery, they were buried in Uncle Andrew's pasture on high ground. I'm sure Mamma is thinking of Papa today too. I'll suggest we take a walk to the graves this evening after supper.

July 22

I'm an aunt! Carrie's daughter Myrtle Elvira was born today. Carrie has been so miserable in this heat, that I'm glad the pregnancy is over. With them living close by, I'm sure we'll see a lot of Myrtle. In between sewing jobs, I've made some tiny clothes out of leftover bits of soft fabric. In this heat, Myrtle isn't going to need much besides a diaper and a short little dress.

August 8

On our way down to the river to fish, we paused a minute to watch the informal baseball game of the neighborhood boys on the school grounds. Eleven-year-old Joseph is going to be in big trouble if Mr. Olson founds out he slipped out of the house on the Sabbath to play ball. Pete Olson is a very religious man that thinks it's a sin to have a good time on Sunday. I don't think he approves of us fishing on Sunday either, but we think of it as resting on the shady river bank rather than getting food for supper. Half the time our bamboo cane poles don't catch a fish anyway.

Family fishing on the banks of the Smoky Hill River

On the way home, we stopped to call on the Oborgs and found out they had bad luck this week. Their milk cow had died in a freak accident. One of Nellie's relation had given them the animal since they couldn't afford to buy one themselves right now. The cow was grazing along the river's edge, must have stretched to reach a high branch of leaves in a tree, slipped and hung itself in the fork of the tree trunk. Its horns got tangled in the branches, and the cow must have broke its neck struggling to get out. Mamma told Nellie she was welcome down to our place to get milk now and then for her two little boys until they get another cow.

September 13

Even though Mr. Lapsley has been bothered by his heart lately, he greeted the children as they entered Star School for the first day of class. When they were all properly welcomed into the new school year, he came over for coffee and *skorpor.* He was tickled that Carrie was over with baby Myrtle. He held her the whole time, telling stories of when Carrie was born twenty years ago.

October 16

Christina and Anna have spent the week with us while Swan is back East on a buying trip. This time with Anna has helped us get to know her, and I think she enjoyed being back out on a farm playing and exploring outdoors. Yesterday we went over to Aunt Magda's to see their new son Elmer who was born two weeks ago. Christina likes to visit around the neighborhood when she gets the chance. Swan drove out to pick up his family this afternoon and told about the new line of buggies and carriages he bought for the implement store on his trip.

November 19

I'm in Assaria sewing winter dresses this month for one of the Peterson families. Wild geese flying south this evening made me homesick for the farm, but I'm enjoying all the activity in town. The Assaria Literary started the fall season last Saturday. This is such a lively group during the program and debate, and with the gossip afterwards.

Last night I attended the magic lantern show of the Holy Land at H. L. Olson's home. I've heard the Bible stories a thousand times, but to see pictures of where life in Biblical times really happened gave me a new perspective.

The news at coffee afterwards was that Dr. Dill disappeared from town without saying goodbye to anyone or paying his bills at the Assaria boarding house. He seemed the perfect gentlemen to me. Why just last week I got my new eye glasses from him.

November 28

Tomorrow, Monday, I go back to Assaria to finish at the Peterson's. I spent the weekend at home since I wasn't there for Thanksgiving. Another week or so and I'll be done with this job and back home for Christmas.

Thursday, after the Thanksgiving service at church and dinner at the Assaria school house, I rode the train with a group of young people to Lindsborg for the Old Settler's of Kansas Concert at Bethany.

Alfred came into Assaria for me Friday evening and I talked him into staying for Dr. Higgins Medicine Show. Besides the usual testimonies to his medicine, he had a monkey that performed tricks for the audience.

Yesterday I rode over to Robinson's to see Mr. Lapsley. He has been so sick that they insisted he move in with them until he's better. He was worried about his few chickens so Mr. Robinson moved them over too. I'm afraid his heart condition isn't going to get any better. They have brought the doctor out several times when Mr. Lapsley's been really bad.

December 2

It was snowing lightly as the crowd waited on the platform for the special train we heard was coming through town. The whole town seems to gather at the depot for important events. After hearing who it was, half the people left, but I waited to see the fancy train cars go by. William Jennings Bryan was passing through Assaria to speak at Lindsborg. Being a Democrat, who ran as the presidential candidate last year, the Assaria people don't think much of him. So no one got excited except Jim Wilson who jumped on the train car and shook Mr. Bryan's hand. You never know who will pass through the big town of Assaria.

December 14

Larry Lapsley, age 57, died yesterday at the Robinsons. He was buried on the Robinson land beside the Robinson boys that never made it through their childhood. Reverend Lockwood of Salina officiated at the funeral. Besides the neighbors at the service, two black men, friends of Mr. Lapsley's from Salina, were present. I was glad I was home for the funeral and so thankful I had visited with him a few weeks ago. He was a special friend to us Swenson children after Papa died. His stories have been heard and cherished by every child in the township. I thought it was fitting that Mr. Lapsley bequeathed his farm to Laura Robinson Hearne, since she taught him to read. Because of the circumstances of his life as a slave growing up in the South, he reminded us whenever possible that education is the key to bettering oneself.

I'll miss taking bread to his home to swap for an apple and an hour of stories.

1898

The Spanish-American War

January 11

Peter Oborg raced along the drifted, snow-covered railroad track to our house early this morning to get help for Gunilla since she had started labor. Mamma straddled behind him on the horse and went back to their farm. Alfred hitched up the team to the buggy for me while I gathered up supplies and food to take over there. I had just finished milking and decided to bring a pail of it along since the Oborgs still haven't gotten another cow. By the time I had driven around the trail to their house, Gunilla was about to deliver their newest child. I fixed the little boys some breakfast of milk gravy and rye bread, which they washed down with a big glass of milk. Peter paced the floor while Elsa Theolinda was born.

January 28

A few of my friends that live close by came over for my birthday coffee yesterday. Most of them are married, and had a baby or two tugging on their skirts as we tried to talk. Since the weather and muddy roads have been bad this month, none of us has ventured into town for supplies or church unless it was absolutely necessary.

Gunilla's mother had been worried because her son-in-law had not brought the baby in to town to be baptized, so Elsa Person arranged that Pastor Wikstrand ride out with her and her husband Theodor this afternoon to baptize the child. While Pastor and Elsa waited at Star School, Theodor walked the tracks down to the Oborg farm. Later we saw the family, all bundled up, walking up the tracks toward the school.

February 10

Peter found another dead hog in the lot this morning. Several neighbors have been losing hogs lately. I wonder if it is damp weather or an outbreak of hog cholera? David Eagles has had bad luck with his hogs too. He lost six pigs when a bank of earth slid down on them the other day.

March 20

Slight rain and a thunder storm passed over our township last Thursday, but the roads were passable to get to church today. Fourth Street in Assaria is lined with blooming trees. Our tree buds at home are just starting to swell.

All anyone could talk about after church was if the United States was going to declare war against Spain. Since Cuba is just ninety miles from Florida, and Americans have considerable money invested in commercial businesses on the island, our country has been pulled into the conflict of the Cuban rebels trying to get their freedom from Spain. Frustrated Spanish soldiers have retaliated against the rebels, who have been burning down the Spanish landlords' buildings and sugar canes, by killing and torturing the Cuban civilians. The U.S. battleship *Maine*, setting in the Havana harbor to protect American interests, blew up mysteriously on February 15th, killing 266 crew members. President McKinley wants to avoid war, but some men in Congress are pressing for it.

People across the nation are already up in arms wanting to help the people on the island. Bridgeport citizens have collected 1350 pounds of flour that will be sent to the starving Cubans next week.

April 9

As we stepped off the train to attend the *Messiah* Days performances, a young college man handed each of us a flyer about an art exhibit in room 112 of the Bethany College building. Everywhere we looked people were being bombarded with the announcement as criers called out the same information. Something important was going on besides the *Messiah* this week. A group of us young neighbors had taken the early train to hear the afternoon concert in the college chapel. The Bethany Band, Norden singing group and soloists gave a nice prelude program for this evening's main concert. Having extra time before the next performance, we lingered over refreshments in the college dining hall and decided to wander over to this art exhibit advertised. I think everyone who got off the train was also curious about the same thing. The place was packed. Professors Birger Sandzen and Carl Lotave had arranged paintings, potting plants and rugs and transformed the classroom into an art gallery. My favorite picture of the show was Sandzen's *Winter Sunset*. Someone ahead of us said they only had one visitor at the art exhibit Wednesday, so the exhibitors decided to boldly advertise today. It worked.

Lindsborg was also talking about the Erickson brothers' newest patent granted this year for a dial telephone. As I understood it, you wind a spring wheel that is attached to the telephone with your finger, and somehow this sends a message down the wires for another phone to ring. John and Carl had a workshop on their farm northeast of Lindsborg and tinkered with the ideas of a horseless buggy, an automatic piano player and a number of other ideas. Five years ago they developed an automatic telephone, then moved to Chicago to work with a telephone company to perfect their invention. Who knows, maybe someday we'll be using these Lindsborg men's inventions.

The chorus of 343 singers did an outstanding job on the *Messiah* rendition. Dr. Olof Olsson was visiting from Illinois and actually stood up during the performance and congratulated the singers on the excellent job they were doing. I bet he never imagined when he organized a small group of people to sing the *Messiah* sixteen years ago that it would swell to the size it is today.

April 25

The United States has officially declared war on Spain! Steel war ships are headed for Cuba. On the other side of the world, Commodore Dewey's Navy fleet stationed at Hong Kong, has been ordered to attack the Spanish fleet sitting in the Manila Bay, in the Philippine Islands. The Congress has asked for the organization of a volunteer army to capture both Cuba and the Philippine Islands. Theodore Roosevelt has resigned his position as Assistant Secretary of the Navy to lead the volunteer cavalry in Cuba. Several Assaria boys are talking of signing up to join his group.

May 7

Attending the circus in Assaria was just the diversion we needed from the war talk. My favorite performances were the trapeze act and an old trick horse. Mabel said several youngsters got duped by the shell game in the side tent. I imagine she was in the thick of things.

May 14

The Star School board called a special meeting this afternoon to decide whether or not to build a larger building. The vote was yes, with the work to be done this summer. Not only has the school gotten too small for the bulging number of students, but it is hardly big enough for community gatherings. Peter is on the building committee along with Uncle Frank, Uncle Nels and Thomas Robb.

May 26

Early summer breezes blew people to Assaria all the way from Lindsborg and Salina for our church picnic today. Besides the talk of the troops landing at Guantanamo Bay in Cuba, talk was on the crops. The wheat heads are starting to fill out and with wheat selling for $1 a bushel, farmers are watching their fields closely. The corn had been going backward because of cold nights, but the weather has changed and it is looking better.

June 18

While I was sitting on the back porch snapping beans this afternoon, I could see Peter weaving through the wheat field, stooping now and then to examine a ripening wheat head. He was on his way back from the school corner. The men have almost finished tearing down the old school house. The good lumber will be used again and the star emblem was saved to be nailed up on the new school. We're not the only school district to think of expansion this year. Assaria voted on a $1,500 bond issue last week for building a high school, but it was voted down.

During supper Peter said he spied black rust on the wheat stems which means the yield will be down. Farming can be so unpredictable. At least with sewing, children grow and clothes wear out, so I will have the seamstress job as long as I want to do it.

July 4

No building being done on the new school house today since everyone has gone to Assaria for the 4th of July celebration. When we went by it today we saw that the belfry is almost done. A play and several box suppers will be held this fall to raise money for the bell. This schoolhouse will be twice the size of the old building, plus a 12 x 12 entry and the belfry.

Besides the usual 4th of July festivities, Assaria had a pole raising today for a new flag bought in Chicago. The flag pole will also be used for weather signals. There was a pretty good crowd, but I think some people went to Salina for the parades and bike races instead.

After the ceremony, war news was announced. The entire Spanish fleet was destroyed by the U.S. ships in the Santiago Bay in Cuba. Land troops, including Teddy Roosevelt's Rough Riders calvary group have stormed San Juan Hill. Because Hawaii proved valuable for a mid-Pacific base for the victory in the Manila Bay, it will be annexed into the United States this next week.

August 14

Spain has sued for peace and negotiations have been under way this month. Spain must agree to withdraw entirely from Cuba, Puerto Rico, West Indies, Guam and the Philippines. Although freedom has been granted to millions of people who were under Spanish rule, it took its toll on the Americans. But of the 5,462 men who died, only 379 were battle related. The other deaths were from malaria and yellow fever. The paper didn't say how many of those who died were from Kansas.

Now that the war is almost over, gossip has turned to local news again. Voices were talking nonstop outside after church this morning. Most of the church members are up against the deacons because the board put out one member for playing a social game of cards. Rumors are that the board secretary has done worse things.

August 22

Peter started plowing the south wheat field today. We had a big rain a week ago last Sunday night that has dried out just right to begin the field work. Also this week a number of boys from Liberty have started work in the McPherson broom factories, too.

The Olsons are raking hay. Seeing them working in the field when I brought out coffee this afternoon to Peter made me think of the time I had an accident while riding the buck rake when I was young. The rake tines hit a rock, lurching the rake and throwing me from the seat. I broke my leg right below the hip. That put an end to field and garden work for me that summer.

Our neighbors, the Olsons putting up hay

September 12

Thirty-nine pupils started class today in the new Star School. Mabel said it just wasn't right without Mr. Lapsley greeting them at the door though. Herman Thorstenberg, their teacher, moved into the little room upstairs yesterday. It seems strange to be older than the teacher.

Sewing jobs around the neighborhood have me booked until Christmas. Pen and ink sketches done by Charles Gibson in *Life* magazine are starting to influence our fashions and the patterns I use. His 'Gibson girl' look of dignified, beautiful clothing, with leg-of-mutton sleeved blouses and gored skirts are catching on in our area. Styles change, sometimes drastically, every year.

November 19

At the box supper tonight a quartette of us girls sang the latest songs, "The Flower That Won My Heart" and "Bring Our Heros

Home" during the program. The socials have been profitable to add needed coffee utensils and dishes to the new school. The coal stove added this winter has warmed up the school house much better than the old stove we used when I was in school. Back then, if we left our lunch pail by the coat rack in the back of the room, our milk was frozen by lunch time.

Star School

December 4

As Pastor read this Sunday's gospel lesson, the altar boy touched the wick of the first white Advent candle with flame from the altar light. The wick flickered, then grew into a strong beam. Each Sunday until Christmas, another candle will be lit until four shine. On Christmas morning, the fifth red candle centered in the ring will be lighted to signify Jesus' birth.

BETHANY COLLEGE,

ORATORIO DEPARTMENT.

January 5th, 1899.
You are most respectfully invited to be a member of the Messiah Chorus of this year. Regular rehearsals Tuesdays at 8 p. m. Sundays 3:30 p. m. First rehearsal January 10th at 7:30 p. m.
CARL SWENSSON, President.
SAMUEL THORSTENBERG,
Conductor.

Invitation to sing in the Messiah

1899

Peter's Brother

January 27

Spent the day of my 26th birthday cutting out material for a blue wool dress for Mrs. Carlson, my Lindsborg employer. This evening I joined some young people I met at *Messiah* practice for an evening of song and entertainment. I wasn't surprised when they brought a birthday cake into the parlor with the coffee. I miss my friends at home, but I am thrilled at being able to work in Lindsborg this winter.

This is my chance to sing in the *Messiah*. I just walk a few blocks from my employer's house to the auditorium. There was no way I could have come into Lindsborg twice a week from home. When I first received the invitation to join the chorus for the performance, I thought it was a joke. But Mr. Carlson assured me that even though Bethany College students make up the majority of the oratorio society, people from the community are welcome too. He heard this was a dream of mine, so he procured an invitation directly from Dr. Swensson himself. I bought the *Messiah* song book at the music store, so I could have a copy of my own. Most of the songs I know by heart since I've heard it many times, but it's different to have to follow a certain melody in your part only. Professor Thorstenberg, our conductor, keeps us on our toes, telling us "to listen to ourselves." Since we have practiced only a few times, we haven't really gone through many songs yet. Some people have sang all seventeen years that the *Messiah* has been sung in Lindsborg. You'd think practice would be boring for them, listening to us first-timers struggle through the difficult passages. But I think the magnetism of the great music pulls them back to sing every year.

February 3

My heart skipped a beat when Willie was ushered into the Carlson home this afternoon. *Farfar* Swen Magnus Anderson died yesterday so he came to bring me home for the funeral. I had just received a letter from Mamma telling me that cousin Carl Brentson, who was a couple years older than me, had died last Saturday and was buried Tuesday. I imagine the blow of losing one of his grandsons was too much for our grandfather.

Farfar was almost 87 years old. I'll miss his stories of his mansion and vast land holdings in Sweden. Ever since *Farfar* and *Farmor* came from the old country, they have had to struggle for what they used to take for granted in Sweden. Land from the King of Sweden had been given to his ancestors many years ago and he had farmers working the land for him. He expected life to be easy in America too, but Kansas soil and weather proved he wasn't cut out to farm his own land. They lived in Minnesota with Uncle Johan Swenson for a while, but moved back to Kansas near us a few winters ago.

March 11

The weather had been warm enough to go outside without a coat, but now winter is back with a vengeance. The temperature plummeted this afternoon as it rained, changed to sleet, then dumped six inches of snow. With the layer of ice underneath, it made walking treacherous for man and beast tonight on Lindsborg's streets.

Work on the new brick factory that A. J. Swanson started building last month here in Lindsborg was halted until warm weather appears again. Besides using the bricks for new buildings, I think it is planned to pave some of the streets of town. With weather like today, bricked paths instead of muddy dirt streets would be much appreciated.

March 29

Silence, a few hushed coughs, then 320 people arose in unison. The violins of the orchestra sweetly set the mood for the first performance. Professor Thorstenborg raised his arms, and the *Messiah* started with "Comfort ye my people saith your God."

I've always wondered what it would be like to sing in the choir instead of listening from the audience. A cold sweat from anticipation has kept me from breathing until the music started. But after we began, I almost forgot the audience, because I was singing for our conductor. But when the audience arose for the "Hallelujah" chorus I knew I was singing for a crowd of four thousand. It was Union Pacific Day and their trains brought people from all along their track to hear us sing. I sung my heart out for these people as I realized one of my dreams had come true. I had sung in the great *Messiah*.

Messiah performance conducted by Prof. Samuel Thorstenberg

March 31

Sitting in the Assaria church tonight, listening to Julia recite her passages for confirmation, I found myself tapping my foot to "For unto us a child is born" from the *Messiah*. The choir would be about at that point in tonight's program. I felt it was more important to be with the family tonight for Julia's confirmation. I'll be singing in the *Messiah* again on Easter Sunday.

Julia's confirmation dress of white satin turned out beautifully. I had finished the Carlson family's sewing a week ago, but they insisted I stay with them until the *Messiah* practice was over. This last week I hand-sewed the lace on Julia's dress for tonight. With her hair up and her body filling out, Julia is becoming a very pretty young lady. Looking at her large class, I realize eleven are from our township. I remember when these children were born, and now they are on the verge of adulthood.

Assaria Confirmation Class— 1899

April 2

From my seat in the chorus, I kept watching for my family to take their places in the auditorium. We came into town together, but after dropping me off at the back door of the auditorium, they went to the train station to meet Peter's brother Nels, who is coming for a visit from Iowa. Peter and his brother have not seen each other since Peter left home twenty-one years ago.

We had just risen for the first number, when my family walked in late to one of the first rows in front of the stage. After Peter scanned the choir, he pointed to me for the stranger next to him. Our eyes met and I was startled at how handsome this gentle-eyed man was. I almost dropped my song book as a slow smile spread on his lips beneath his brown mustache. This was my stepfather's brother, Nels.

April 13

I'm so glad I wasn't sewing for someone these past two weeks. I don't know what I would have done if I wasn't home during Nels' visit. Mamma finally commented last night that Nels came to Kansas to visit Peter, not me. Nels and I have walked down to the river, taken buggy rides to see the countryside and have talked about everything under the sun. Last evening as we rocked slowly in the porch swing, he asked if he could write to me after he went back to Iowa. I wish he lived near here because I think I've fallen in love. This is the man I've been waiting for the past ten years, but with my luck he lives in Iowa, and he's my step-uncle.

Before Nels boarded the train this morning, he pressed his calling card in my hand and squeezed it tightly. He started to board his car, then hesitated, jumped back down and kissed me! Just that quick he was back on the train as it started to move away from the depot. My first romantic kiss was in front of my stepfather, by his forty-year-old brother!

April 15

Fire struck downtown Lindsborg last night destroying Roseberg's furniture store, Holmgren's meat market and Thorstenberg's music store. All the handsome furniture and beautiful instruments I looked at through the store windows as I shopped downtown this winter are reduced to ashes. How quickly a single spark can change someone's livelihood.

May 23

The worst storm in our county's history struck yesterday about 5 p.m. Volumes of rolling dust, roaring like a locomotive toward the farm, sent us running to the cellar. The front of stinging rain and hail hit with gale force. We didn't have time to latch the barn door, let alone close the windows upstairs in our bedrooms. The force of the wind and rain blew the chickens in the air like single feathers. Never had I remembered hail so large. After an hour and a half, the front rumbled on to the south to do more destruction. Shredded curtains flapped out of broken windows on the north and west sides of the house. The hail had pulverized the screens and broken the windows. Shingles and siding looked like someone had taken vengeance on our house with a hammer. All the buildings were damaged and the crops were mutilated.

News of the destruction traveled through the area as neighbors traveled to other farms to see who needed the most help. The area of devastation covered an area from Brookville to Lindsborg. Many farms lost fruit trees and grape vines and of course the wheat and alfalfa fields were broken into short green stubble. Salemsborg Church was damaged. Uncle Claus Sjogren's elevator was wrecked at Smolan. Nearly every window in Assaria and Bridgeport was broken and a number of people were seriously hurt. In downtown Lindsborg, the large windows of the Brunswick Hotel were blown out and Grondal's gallery was damaged. The tin sheeting was torn off a good part of the Ladies Dormitory roof at Bethany College. Wet plaster ceilings fell in the top rooms from water damage. The destruction of this disastrous storm will affect everyone for the rest of the year as they repair buildings and plow under their ruined crops.

June 16

Now that we are getting our mail delivered to the farm through Mr. Ericson, the rural carrier, I think the whole neighborhood knows when I get a letter. I beat Mabel to the mailbox this morning, but Mr. Ericson slowly thumbed through our mail, knowing I wanted to get my hands on it. "Well, well, I believe there's another letter from Iowa for Miss Alma Swenson. I see your suitor spells his last name with two n's instead of one like Peter. These letters seem to be coming fairly regular these days," he said with a knowing smile.

I stuffed my new letter in my apron pocket and walked out to the garden instead of back to the house.

Sliding down the trunk of the apple tree I opened his latest letter. Nels writes the most wonderful letters. He mainly writes what he's doing on his farm—describing his acres or the orneriness of one of his horses. I guess it's what's between the lines that I love the most. I can tell he cares for me and is thinking of me even while he's milking his cow or working the field near his house.

At first I hesitated to write back, afraid I would encourage him. Why should I carry on a romance through the mail to a man in another state? But I thought of our eyes meeting during the *Messiah* and I knew I must write back to Nels. I wish he lived in the next county instead of two states away though.

July 4

We joined the bustling celebration in crowded Assaria today. Over two thousand people mingled in the streets, paused to watch the children play games and listen to the speeches and bands. As soon as we pulled into town, we scattered in different directions. Mamma and Peter listened to the orations by R. L. Head and R. P. Cravens, both prominent men from Salina. Alfred and Willie watched the ball game between Assaria and Smolan. Julia found Millie in the crowd and went to look at the exhibits.

Hilda Olson finally talked Mabel into entering the sack races. Since Minnie Granquist was home for a visit, Mabel was questioning her on Kansas City dress fashions. She's starting to like clothes and doesn't think my 'Bridgeport fashions' are the up and coming thing. After Mabel and Hilda ran off, we found a shady spot in the church grove and caught up on secrets. I found out that while I've been writing to Nels, brother Willie has been writing to Minnie. I got the impression that their childhood friendship might be turning into a romantic one.

July 17

Nellie Oborg gave birth to their latest child, Philip Emanuel, today. She's a hard worker, but repairing the damaged buildings and garden on their place, while being very pregnant have taken it's toll on her. She has her hands full now with four children all under the age of four. We made extra for dinner today and I walked to Oborgs with the food later.

August 25

As I sat on the south porch this evening, watching the barn swallows dip down to tease the cats, Mabel asked for another piece of writing paper. She and Hilda are always writing notes back and forth that they send with whoever is going to one farm or the other. Before she interrupted my daydreaming, I was trying to think what else to write to Nels. Mostly I've written of the everyday events going on this summer as we work the fields and garden. What's the latest news in Bridgeport or who stopped by to visit. Since Nels has been here, he can see in his mind the person, creek or town I'm talking about. I have to envision his world only by his descriptions and my imagination. I wonder if I'll ever get the chance to visit his farm and his and Peter's family in Iowa.

September 18

Another school year starts as the bell clangs in the belfry of Star. Mr. Francis Robb is the school master for 37 students this fall. Some of the older boys won't show up until winter has set in. Due to the farm work, they only get half the days in that the girls and younger students do. The harvest comes first.

September 27

I rode the train into Salina Monday to spend a few days with Christina since the railroad is running at half price during the Saline County Fair. Yesterday we sat on the street curb, watching the parade with all the fancy floats and bands. In the afternoon we moseyed through the exhibits of handiwork, baked goods, and prize animals. Anna wanted to see the amusements so we walked through the Midway in Rosedale Park. Swan went with us for the evening performance in Oak Dale Park. The "Battle of Manila" was performed by 300 people, followed by a fireworks display.

I told Christina about Nels' frequent letters. She said, "Don't worry about what Mamma or Peter might say, just follow your heart."

September 31

Gossip was buzzing before church instead of waiting until afterwards today. Last night someone dynamited the Assaria Post Office that's located in the back of C. G. Johnson's store. The safe and fixtures were blown to pieces. Of course it woke up half the town, but before the dust cleared the bandits took off with $150 worth of stamps, $185 of government money and $50 of the postmaster's money. That's the second time the post office has been robbed recently and neither crime has been solved.

October 22

Good-byes were said today to Mrs. Bryngelson, who was Peter Olson and Aunt Magda's mother. Service was held at Aunt Magda's farm, where her mother has lived for the past eleven years. Wagons of solemn neighbors followed the casket's wagon to the Assaria cemetery. Mrs. Bryngelson is almost the last of the original group of relatives in our extended family that followed their children to America. Sometimes I'm amazed at the changes I've seen in my lifetime. Think of the changes she saw in her 83 years.

December 9

I read in this week's newspaper that Dr. Olof Olsson, the pioneer that started Bethany Church and the College died in Rock Island, Illinois, last Saturday. There was a big write up about the accomplishments of his life, both as a pioneer in this area and his work at the Augustana College in Illinois.

December 25

I don't really believe my wish about Nels will come true, but when Mabel put the *pepparkakor* in my hand, I had to try. On Christmas day, you put the cookie in the palm of your hand, make a wish, then tap in the center of the cookie. If the *pepparkakor* breaks into three pieces, your wish will come true. Luck was with me!

Then I found the almond in my serving of Christmas *rispudding*. Everyone knows that means the finder will marry within the year. What will the year 1900 in the new century have in store for me?

Wedding picture of Minnie Granquist and Willie Swenson

1900

Wedding Bells

January 27

Instead of "Happy Birthday" written on the bottom of my birthday card from Nels, I stared at his handwritten "Will you marry me?" I closed my eyes and opened them again, thinking the words would change, but they didn't. How can I describe the feelings fluttering in my chest? For years I've longed for the moment when the right man would kneel down at my feet and ask me that question. But I always assumed it would be someone I had grown up with in the neighborhood and that I would settle on a farm near my childhood home.

I am twenty-seven years old today. Nels is forty. I wish we had met ten years ago when I wouldn't have thought so much about leaving the farm. As I get older, this homestead grows more dear to me. But if I want to be with the man I love, I'm going to have to leave Kansas.

February 19

Cyrene Jane Smith, Mrs. Robinson's step-mother, died of rheumatism of the heart this week. She was laid to rest in the burial plot on the Robinson place.

When you're a child you think everything stays the same. But in reality people grow old, farms change hands, and people you've known forever move away. Will today's neighborhood children remember me after I move to Iowa, or will I just be a fading memory of "one of the Swenson girls that left the farm"?

Another change will happen in our family this year. Willie has asked for Minnie's hand in marriage. She'll soon move back from Kansas City to plan their June wedding.

March 9

When Alfred brought in eggs to sell today, the store keeper told Alfred he really needed them. Gypsies camped by Bridgeport this last week because of the driving snow from our late storm. After the wanderers moved on, chickens and eggs were discovered missing around town.

April 15

What a terrible week for the *Messiah*. I'm glad I decided not to try to get to practices from the country this year because the weather this week has been too bad to get to the performances.

This year, due to the increase in the amount of people wanting to see the *Messiah*, the performances were increased to four nights. It even got national attention with an article in the April issue of the *Ladies Home Journal*.

The *Lindsborg Record* reports that Tuesday the performers and audiences had to fight a blinding snowstorm to attend. Wednesday's performance was cut down by the biting cold, with mud and water standing in puddles everywhere. At least Friday the sun shone so people took advantage of the day. The eighteen coaches coming from the south were so overloaded it took the Union Pacific engine over an hour to haul the train up from McPherson. Today on Easter Sunday it is pouring rain. The black cloud has hung around all day. I'm sure it has been a difficult performance with the heavy air wet and echoless, and the choir competing with the rhythm of the rain on the round roof of the auditorium.

May 12

Mamma hosted the Women's Missionary Society at our house today. The conversation while stitching on our church projects was on the family weddings coming up soon. Even though the talk was about me and the sewing progress of my wedding clothes, I'd rather have escaped the house to reread my morning mail. If the ladies only knew Nels' latest letter was tucked inside my good apron pocket, they probably would have wanted me to read it out loud. I would die of embarrassment if they knew the sweet things he said in this letter. I couldn't keep my thoughts on Christian missionary work this afternoon no matter how hard I tried.

June 6

Carrie Nation's battle against Kansas joints and drug stores that sell illegal liquor hit the front page of the newspaper today. Earlier this summer she successfully closed such businesses in Medicine Lodge where she lives. This month Kiowa became her target. Armed with a buggy of fist-sized rocks, this six foot, 175-pound women reduced three joints to splintered shambles while patrons hid under tables. No gilded mirror, bottle or plate glass store window was left intact after she was through. I wonder what town will become her next target.

June 12

My best friend Minnie Granquist became my sister-in-law today as she married brother Willie. Reverend Pihlblad, the assistant pastor of Bethany Church, officiated the service in the parlor of her parents' home. Her sisters prepared a huge meal for the large crowd of relatives and guests that mingled on the lawn after the wedding. The most polite shivaree party I've ever encountered, serenaded the couple with mandolins and guitars after they asked Mr. Granquist's permission. I hope we're lucky to have an orderly group when my wedding takes place in a few months.

June 13

Willie is working beside Peter and Alfred in the wheat field this afternoon as if it was just another day. It has been an early harvest, so no honeymoon yet for Willie and Minnie. I helped Minnie and her sisters haul her things to the farmhouse north of us that Willie has been living in this year.

June 23

On our way into Assaria this evening we stopped at the cemetery grave of Robert Wheeler to pay our respects. Our 58-year-old neighbor died Wednesday of cancer of the stomach. Mr. Wheeler, his wife and eight children have been a part of our township for 30 years. The community of Wheeler School, which was named after him, will miss his help and support.

With the wheat cut, we ventured into town to hear the band concert that's held on Saturday nights in the City Square during the summer. There were so many people in town from the country that we had a hard time finding a hitching post for our team.

July 17

The *Lindsborg Record* has a column on Assaria and Bridgeport happenings each week. If we haven't heard about something from a neighbor or from someone in town, we'll find out about it in the paper. James Smith, who lives a half mile north of Assaria, lost 4 stacks of wheat (1,500 bushels) to fire Monday. He was burning the stubble on the edge of the field and the fire got away.

We knew that thieves broke into the Fagerburg's store in Bridgeport last week and stole $75 worth of goods. The newspaper reported that Ed Carlson was arrested this week for the theft.

J. R. Bazeman, who runs the mills in Bavaria and Bridgeport, is building a plant at Assaria.

News that our church was hit by lightning last week also made the newspaper. Fortunately, the damage was slight to the steeple, instead of burning the church down to the ground. We saw the damage when we went to church Sunday. The point of the belfry was splintered and fried black. Thank goodness heavy rains put the fire out right away.

Reading the newspaper and knowing the area so well that the stories are about, has made me face the worry that has been nagging my mind lately. This fall I am moving to a foreign place, where I won't know the neighbors, the shopkeepers, the congregation or the farmland. Will I be able to adapt to my new surroundings and its people?

This summer as I pull weeds in the garden, ladle boiling currant jelly into the scalded jars, or snap beans for our dinner while sitting on the south porch, I keep thinking this is the last season I'll do this task on this farm. I know every inch of this house—how the attic door creaks like a ghost is rattling the latch, to how many pint jars fit on the third shelf in the cellar. We carved our names into the new wood in the hayloft when the barn was built, and I've spent countless hours in the stalls milking the cows and grooming the horses. I could walk to the south meadow blindfolded, knowing where to cross the creek and find the cows because of the lifetime trips to that pasture since childhood. How long is it going to take me to feel this much at home on the new farm in Iowa?

August 13

Yards of white satin and lace trim have covered the stretched quilt stand set up in the parlor this month as I work on my wedding gown. I've had quilts and linens stored away for my new home for years, but now we're getting my clothing made.

Carrie was sitting on the floor marking the hem of my wedding gown when she announced, with a mouth full of pins, that she is expecting another baby next spring. Of course I was happy, but I felt a wave of guilt and sadness because I won't be here to help her. It could be years before I'm back home to meet my new niece or nephew.

Marriage License of Nels Runneberg and Alma Swenson

August 30

My groom arrived today! Since we had to apply for our marriage license at the county seat, I rode the train and met Nels in Salina. After a trip to the courthouse, we caught the next train to Bridgeport.

It's been over a year since I saw my fiance, but I've seen his face in my mind everyday. It felt awkward to think I'm going to be intimate on our wedding night and the rest of my life with a man I've only spent a few weeks with over a year ago. But in my heart I know him through his letters and I believe we will be happy together.

The house has been in turmoil this week. I've been finishing last minute details on my sewing. Julia and Mabel have been cleaning house. Alfred raked the yard and cleaned out the flower beds I've neglected this fall as I sewed my wedding dress. Now that Nels is here, I seem to float above the work, not doing my share. But Mamma shooed me out of the house tonight to take a long walk with Nels instead of doing the supper dishes. She understands we need time alone.

September 5

After Mamma left my room, I stood at the top of the stairs listening to Julia play the piano downstairs in the parlor. Mabel stood behind me, holding up my veil, ready to make the descent. The sweet fragrance of the orange blossoms tucked into my bouquet of white chrysanthemums scented the stairwell. I knew when I walked down those stairs life would never be the same. I would not be the girl that grew up in this house, but a married woman with a house of my own in Iowa that I have not yet seen.

When I got to the bottom of the stairs and walked through the dining room, all eyes were on me as my relatives and friends parted to make a path to the parlor. Nels and Reverend Wistrand turned from their post in the southeast corner of the room as I paused at the threshold. Drifting into the room, with my eyes only on Nels, I knew I was doing the right thing. As the mantle clock struck 3:30, Pastor began reading the wedding vows from his book. I was nervous enough to hardly remember most of Wistrand's words, but I remember Nels' declaration of love when he placed the wide gold band on my ring finger. Inside the ring it is etched "Nels and Alma, 9-5-1900." I am now Mrs. Nels Runneberg.

The plank tables and chairs borrowed from the school house were set up on the east lawn of the house for the wedding supper. The last tomatoes I'll ever grow here were served with a bounty of food from our farm: chicken, fresh beef, potatoes, currant jelly on wheat bread. Yesterday Mamma, Carrie and Minnie spent the day making pies and bread in each of their kitchens. Mamma and my sisters did a lot of work to prepare the meal for our many guests. After everyone had eaten their fill, we opened the many wedding gifts our family had showered on us. My favorites were the crystal bowls and vases, although we need all of the useful presents too. We'll have several trunks of carefully packed presents to ship to Iowa. Next summer I'll arrange flowers from my new garden in the cut glass vases and remember this day. Before we left the farm for the Brunswick Hotel in Lindsborg, we heard singing voices mixed with wagon wheels and harnesses coming from the south. Friends from Bridgeport came to serenade us to our honeymoon!

Nels and Alma Runneberg

September 12

This last week we have been isolated in Lindsborg, sleeping late, spending idle time sitting on a bench in Bethany Park or walking along the edge of the Smoky Hill River down by the mill. This was our time to get to know each other, away from our family and farm work.

We had to emerge today for another wedding in the neighborhood. Måns Peterson's son, Charles, wed Pete and Hannah Olson's daughter, Alma, today. After the wedding supper at the Peterson home, they moved to their new farm northwest of Hallville.

I think Nels and I held hands the whole day except when we were eating. I blushed when anyone asked us about the honeymoon. If they knew what went on in our honeymoon suite I'd be scarlet-faced forever!

September 21

This week we've stayed on the farm. Life almost seems back to normal except I am in bed with Nels instead of a sister.

This morning before they starting chopping silage, the men drove a herd of fatted steers up to the railroad pens at Hallville to be shipped to Kansas City to be sold. Our animals, along with those of neighbors, filled nine carloads on the train. The cattle going by the farm reminded me of the longhorn cattle days, when huge herds would go by the farm and the school house. Usually a rider would go ahead of the herd to warn the farmers and teacher if possible. We didn't dare go outside until the mass of cattle had trampled through the school yard. Rows of hedge trees around the farmers' fields gave some protection to the crops. Papa would line the wagons across our driveway to deter the longhorns from running into the farm yard.

While Nels helped Peter, I packed our wedding gifts and my belongings for the trip to Iowa. I've been packing our presents in with the new linen and dresses that I made for my trousseau. The glass and china pieces are wrapped in petticoats and layered in the quilts. I worry if the thin etched water glasses will make the trip. Will there still be twelve intact when we get to Iowa? The cranberry-colored lead crystal bowl would look pretty in our parlor here. I wonder where I'll put it in my new house?

One of Mamma's presents, "from the farm," as she put it, was several cases of canned fruit, vegetables and jelly that we put up this summer. I wondered why with only five left in the family this winter, we needed to put up so much food. I guess I didn't think that Nels being a bachelor wouldn't have a cellar stocked with preserved garden produce. Whenever I open up a jar to use, I'll close my eyes and see the tree or garden row it came from.

Tucked in one corner of a trunk is a copy of the September 14th *Lindsborg Record* newspaper that carried our wedding announcement. Unfortunately our little article was overshadowed by the gruesome news of 3,000 people that died in the Galveston, Texas, flood last week. I shudder to think of what I would do if anything would happen to Nels.

September 27

All of our family plus most of Bridgeport was on the train for Salina early this morning to go to the Salina Street Fair. Buffalo Bill's Wild West Show lead by Colonel Cody himself performed today. His show has played for kings and queens all over the world since it was started in '83. Fifty-two railroad cars for the traveling exhibition were sitting on side tracks near the depot. We couldn't believe the crowds when we got off the train. Later I heard that there were 27,000 paid admissions for the show. The day started with a parade downtown of the cowboys, Indians and animals that performed later in the show. Buffalo Bill, leading the procession, dressed in a decorated buckskin suit, sat tall in the saddle on his white steed. Cody's long mane of hair blew in the breeze under his Stetson as he waved and smiled at the crowds. Just after he passed us, I noticed someone step out of the crowd and reach out his hand. Colonel Cody reached down and shook hands with Uncle Ola Peterson!

The show was a kaleidoscope of events that was meant to portray life on the frontier and beyond. The action happened so fast, one act after another, that I dared not blink. Re-enactment of historic Indian and army clashes, complete with tepees, bugle-blaring chargers and female captives to be rescued, caused us to sit on the edge of our seats for fear the winners of the battle would attack the crowd next. Like a bolt of lightning the pony express riders flashed by the stands as they raced to exchange horses and the sacred saddle bag of mail. Hollering cowboys chased a herd of longhorn cattle while at the other end of the arena, a band of Indians pursued a deafening stampede of buffalo. Trying to ride bucking broncos and rope steers caused many cowboys to hit the dirt. The huge crowd hushed as an Indian slowly slipped towards an elk herd, bow and arrow posed for a mock kill. Precision drill teams from Germany, Russia, Mexico and France, all in their native army costumes, and members from Roosevelt's Rough

Riders from the Spanish-American War paraded their specialties. Nels' favorite scene was the assault on the Deadwood stage coach. Going full blast with Indians in pursuit, firing guns in the air, the passengers were literally hanging on for their lives. I think the best act was Annie Oakley. Whether it was shooting a cigarette out of her husband's mouth, a dime between his fingers, or snuffing out the flames on a rapidly revolving wheel of candles, I can see where she got the nickname "Little Sure Shot." She started the riding part of her act by leaping on her pony as it came galloping into the arena, scooping her pistol out of the grass and firing on six glass balls that had been thrown in the air at the same time. As long as I live, I will never forget this spectacular day.

September 29

Christina surprised Nels at breakfast with a cake for his 41st birthday. We're staying with Christina's this week while we visit the fair.

We heard a spirited speech by New York's Governor Teddy Roosevelt last night. He is campaigning across the nation for the Republican ticket as vice-president for William McKinley. He was also scheduled to speak briefly in Ling Auditorium on the way through Lindsborg.

Today's fair theme, the Festival of Republican Prosperity, featured Governor Stanley and Senator Hanna as speakers. It was our last chance to explore the exhibits. I could have spent half my day watching the glass blowing demonstration, but Nels wanted to check out the crop winners to see what variety of wheat and corn got the top premiums. The exploding fireworks after the outdoor moving picture show tonight was the perfect ending to our stay in Salina.

September 30

Saying too many good-byes today has saddened me to the point of tears several times. Early this morning, Swan, Christina and Anna drove us to Assaria Church in the surrey. We were the last to leave the church yard after services because there were so many people who wanted to wish me farewell. I used several more handkerchiefs when Christina's family disappeared down the road this afternoon. When will I see my older sister again?

October 1

I rose early this morning, leaving Nels in bed. I wanted to walk around the farm one more time, before we take the train to Iowa today. I peeked in at the sleeping hens on their roost in the chicken house. The confused rooster ruffled his feathers, knowing it wasn't quite time to pronounce his morning call. Wandering into the barn I could smell the last crop of alfalfa in the haymow, feel the vibration of the draft horses stamping their feet and hear the milk cows chewing their cud. Feeling the rough wooden boards of the inside wall, I confidently tiptoed in the dark to the third buffalo horn and took down the bridle. Once I was back outside, old Bonnie nickered softly in the pen. Riding bareback in the first light, we toured the fields ready to be harvested, waded the shallow creek in the meadow and ended up in Andrew's pasture beside my father's grave. From the top of the hill I watched the sun rise and heard the world awaken.

Mamma found me this morning, shovel in hand, my tears dripping on my double pink peony bush as I pried it from the earth. I had to take something with me that had grown in the soil of this farm. Mamma understood. She had felt the same way when she left Sweden and her family to follow the man she loved. Mamma handed me the uprooted plant and with tears in her own eyes, said, "You will be homesick for us and this farm, but my prayers and your book of memories will help you remember your life here. Go start your new life with your husband. Your prairie is waiting."

Nels and Alma Runneberg

Swedish Glossary

farfar: paternal grandfather
farmor: paternal grandmother
fruktsoppa: dried fruit cooked into a soup
Gud Hjalper: book title, *God's Help*
Hosianna: name of the Swedish song, "Hosanna"
I Lifvets Vår: Book title, *In the Spring of Life*
Julafton: Christmas Eve
Julotta: Early morning Christmas church service
ljuskrona: means lighted crown, a Christmas candelabra
      with candles on the end of the branches
lutfisk: dried stockfish, soaked, then cooked
ostkaka: a custard dessert or cheesecake
pepparkakor: ginger or molasses cookies
potatiskorv: sausage made with ground meat,
      onions, potatoes and spices
prärieblomman: prairie flower
rispudding: cooked rice pudding
skorpor: rusks, dried bread with cinnamon and sugar
smörbakelser: butter cookies
smörgåsbord: variety of foods served buffet style
spritz: a delicate butter cookie
tack så mycket: thank you very much

Standing: Maria and Andrew Johnson, Emma and Frank Fager
Seated: Claus and Sara Sjogren, Peter and Kajsa Runeberg

Standing: Julia, Alfred, Christina and Carrie
Seated: Alma, Willie and Mabel

Family Chart

Johan Magnus and Anna Lisa Andreasson
(Alma's maternal grandparents)
Their children:
1. Erick Johanson, married Magdalena Olson in 1883.
    children: Emelia, Hulda, Martin
2. Anna Sara, married Claus Sjogren in 1872.
    children: Oscar, Phena, Emma, Carl, Selma
3. *Maja Kajsa, married Carl Swenson in 1866.*
    children: Christina, Wilhelm, Alma, Alfred, Carrie
    Maja Kajsa married Peter Runeberg in 1883.
    children: Julia and Mabel
4. Andrew Johnson, married Maria Petersson in 1881.
    children: Emelia (Millie)
5. Emma, married Frank Fager in 1878, no children.

Sven Magnus and Katarina Andersson
(Alma's paternal grandparents)
Their children:
1. Maja Lena, married Olof Danielsson.
    children: Anna, Karl, Alfrida, Albin, Sven, Aron, Klara
2. *Carl Johan Svensson, married Maja Kajsa Johansdotter.*
    children: listed above
3. Anna Kajsa, married Edvin Johnson.
    children: Clara, Johan, Denius, Severin, Matilda, Axel
    Anna Kajsa married Ola Peterson in 1877.
    children: Ida, Selma, Hilma, Hilegard, Karl, Gertrude
4. Sara Lisa, married Johannes Brentson.
    children: Anna, Carolina, Karl, William, Johannes, Emma, Gustaf, Elizabeth, Emanuel
5. Anders Magnus Svensson (died in Sweden)

6. Clara Christina, married Otto Peterson in 1869.
   children: Gustaf, August, Emma, Selma, Beda,
   Victoria, Hilma
7. Emma Katarina, married Sven Carlberg.
   children: Julia, Ernest, Olga, Agnes, Bror, Sven
8. Emanuel Edvin Swenson, married Hannah Hanson.
   children: Millie, Karl, Lydia, Klara, Blenda, Vera, Otto
9. Johan Wilhelm Swenson, married Eva Peterson in 1882.
   children: Emelie, Olive, Ellen, Amanda, Ida, Julia,
   Leonard, Eva, Elmer, Clarence
10. Elenora Matilda, married Charley Fairchild.
    children: Walter, Gilbert, Mildred, Chauncy

Olof and Kajsa Bryngelson
(Second cousins on both mother's and father's side)
Their children:
1. Peter Olson, married Hannah Carlson in 1875.
   children: Hilda, Alma, Emma, Joseph, Hilda,
   Gottfrid, Alviria, Carl
2. Magdalena, married Erick Johanson in 1883.
   children: see above
   Magdalena married Nels G. Johnson in 1893.
   children: Arthur, Elmer
3. Cathrina Anna

Footnote: You may have noticed several variations of last names among these families. It was the Swedish custom to take the father's first name as the child's last name. So Johan Magnus Andreasson's children would be Erick Johanson (Johan's son) and Maja Kajsa Johansdotter (Johan's daughter).

Changing the spelling of a Swedish name to the American version was very common. For example, Andrew Johnson's Swedish name was Anders Johanson. The names Andreasson and Andersson became Anderson and Svensson changed to either Swenson or Swanson.

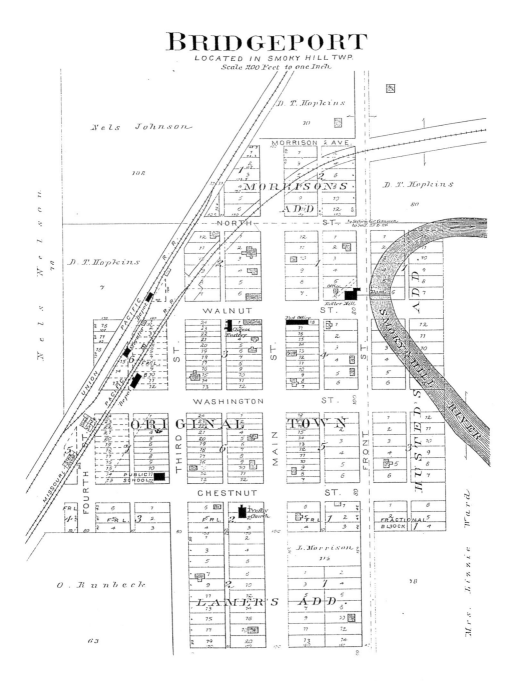

1903— *Bridgeport, Kansas*

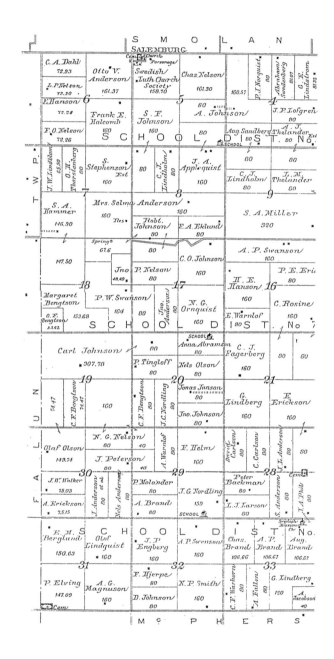

1903— Saline County, Kansas

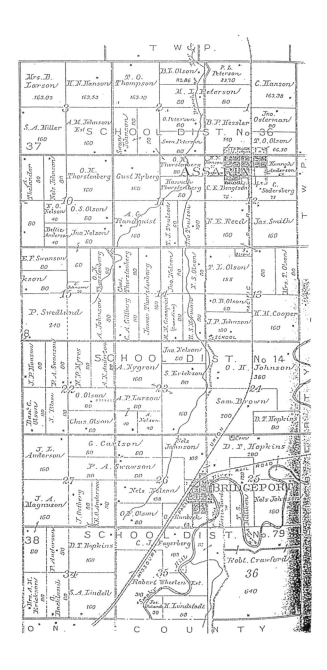

Township 16 South. Range 3 West.

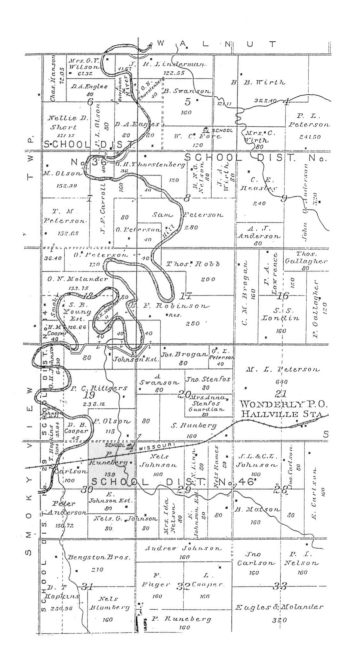

1903— Saline County, Kansas

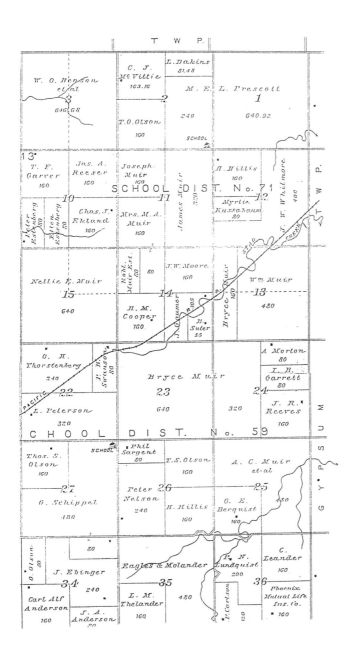

Township 16 South. Range 2 West.

1903— Assaria, Kansas

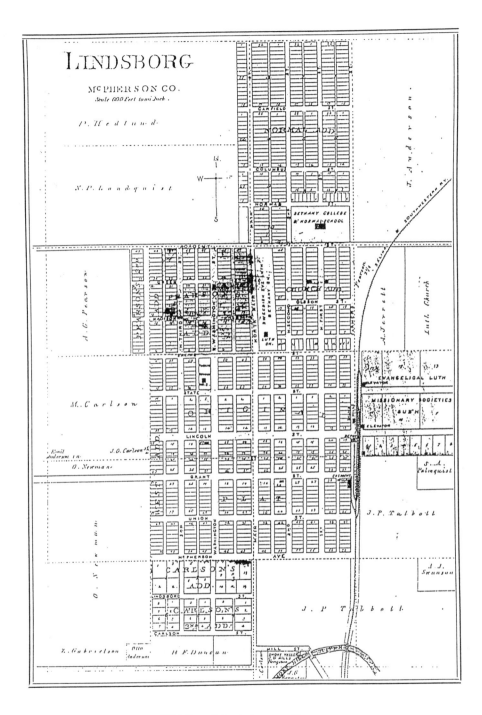

1886— Lindsborg, Kansas

Order Form

Book Kansas!/Butterfield Books
P.O. Box 407
Lindsborg, KS 67456
1-800-790-2665

SEND TO:

Name _____

Address _____

City _____

State _____ Zip _____

Phone # _____

❏ Check enclosed for entire amount payable to
  Butterfield Books

❏ Visa   ❏ MasterCard

Card # ❏❏❏❏ ❏❏❏❏ ❏❏❏❏ ❏❏❏❏

Exp Date ❏❏

Signature (or call to place your order) _____ Date _____

ISBN #	TITLE	QTY	UNIT PRICE	TOTAL
1-886652-00-7	Butter in the Well		9.95	
1-886652-01-5	Prärieblomman		9.95	
1-886652-02-3	Egg Gravy		9.95	
1-886652-03-1	Looking Back		9.95	
1-886652-04-X	**Cassette:** Butter in the Well		9.95	
1-886652-05-8	**Cassette:** Prärieblomman		9.95	
	Note cards: Butter in the Well		4.95	
	Note cards: Homestead		4.95	
	Postcards: Homestead		3.95	
1-886652-06-6	Trail of Thread		9.95	
1-886652-07-4	Thimble of Soil		9.95	
1-886652-08-2	Stitch of Courage		9.95	
			Subtotal	
	CO residents add 7.55% and KS add 6.4% tax			
	Shipping & Handling: per address ($3.00 for first item. Each additional item .50)			
			Total	

Retailers and Libraries: Books are available through Butterfield Books, B & T, Booksource, Ingram and Pacific Pipeline.
RIF Programs and Schools: Contact Butterfield Books for discount, ordering and author appearances.

Bibliography

PUBLISHED MATERIAL

40th Anniversary Album of the Evangelical Lutheran Congregation of Salemsborg, 1869-1959.

100th Anniversary Yearbook, Bethany Lutheran Church, Lindsborg, Kansas. Wichita, Kansas: Jeffery's of Kansas, 1969.

Adams, James Truslow, ed. *Album of American History. Vol. 3, 1853-1893* and *Vol. 4, 1893-1917.* New York: Charles Scribner's Sons, 1946.

Allender, Etta Wallace. *A History of One-room Public Schools of Saline County, Kansas.* 1992.

Anderson, E.T. *A Quarter-inch of Rain.* Wichita, Kansas: McCormick-Armstrong Co. Inc., 1962.

Assaria, Kansas, 80th Anniversary, 1886-1966.

Baughman, Robert W. *Kansas Post Offices: May 29, 1828 to August 3, 1961.* Topeka, Kansas: The Kansas State Historical Society, 1961.

Billdt, Ruth. *Pioneer Swedish-American Culture in Central Kansas.* Lindsborg, Kansas: Lindsborg News-Record, 1965.

Billdt, Ruth, and Jaderborg, Elizabeth. *The Smoky Valley in the After Years.* Lindsborg, Kansas: Lindsborg News-Record, 1969.

Blackstone, Sarah J. *The Business of Being Buffalo Bill.* New York: Praeger Publishers, 1988.

Building by Faith, from yesterday . . . for tomorrow. The Assaria Luterhan Church, Assaria, Kansas 1875-1975. Lindsborg, Kansas: Lindsborg News-Record, 1975.

Burke, John. *Buffalo Bill, The Noblest Whiteskin.* New York: G. P. Putnam's Sons, 1973.

Chrisman, Harry E. *The 1,001 Most-asked Questions about the American West.* Athens, Ohio: Swallow Press, 1982.

Collins, David R. *Grover Cleveland.* Ada, Okla.: Garrett Educational Corporation, 1988.

Collins, David R. *William McKinley.* Ada, Okla.: Garrett Educational Corportation, 1990.

Cordier, Mary Hurlbut. *Schoolwomen of the Prairies and Plains.* Albuquerque: The University of New Mexico Press, 1992.

Cunningham, Robert E. *Indian Territory.* Norman, Okla.: University of Oklahoma Press, 1957.

Deaths and Interments- Saline Co., Kansas 1859-1985. Compiled by the Smoky Valley Genealogical Society and Library Inc., 1985.

Eiseman, Alberta. *From Many Lands.* New York: Atheneum, 1970.

Ellis, Anne. *Plain Anne Ellis.* Lincoln, Neb.: University of Nebraska Press, First Bison Book printing, Feb. 1984.

Hicks, John D., Mowry, George E. and Burke, Robert E. *The American Nation.* Fifth Edition. Boston: Houghton Mifflin Company, 1971.

Horan, James David. *The Authentic Wild West.* New York: Crown Publishers, Inc., 1977.

Jensen, Richard E., Paul, R. Eli and Carter, John E. *Eyewitness at Wounded Knee.* Lincoln, Neb.: University of Nebraska Press, 1991.

Johnson, Maurine. *Swedish Footprints on the Kansas Prairie.* Hillsboro, Kansas: Multi Business Press, 1993.

Jones, Virgil Carrington. *Roosevelt's Rough Riders.* New York: Doubleday & Company, Inc., 1971.

Koch, William E. *Folklore from Kansas: Customs, Beliefs, and Superstitions.* Lawrence, Kansas: The Regents Press of Kansas, 1980.

Lamer, Howard R. *The Reader's Encyclopedia of the American West.* New York: Thomas Y. Crowell Company, 1977.

Levitt, Sarah. *Victorians Unbuttoned: Registered Designs for Clothing, their Makers and Wearers, 1839-1900.* London: George Allen & Unwin, 1986.

Liman, Ingemar. *Traditional Festivities in Sweden.* Stockholm: The Swedish Institute, 1991.

Lindquist, Emery. *Bethany in Kansas: The History of a College.* Lindsborg, Kansas: Bethany College Publications, 1975.

Lindquist, Emory. *The Smoky Valley People: A History of Lindsborg, Kansas.* Rock Island, Ill.: Augustana Book Concern, 1953.

Lindsborg Efter Femtio År. Rock Island, Ill.: Augustana Book Concern, 1919.

Lindsborg pa Svensk-Amerikansk Kulturbild från Mellersta Kansas. Rock Island, Ill.: Augustana Book Concern, 1909.

Madison, Arnold. *Carry Nation.* Nashville: Thomas Nelson Inc., Publishers, 1977.

Marrin, Albert. *The Spanish-American War.* New York: Antheneum, 1991.

McGill, Allyson. *The Swedish Americans.* New York: Chelsea House Publishers, 1988.

McReynolds, Edwin C. *Oklahoma: A History of the Sooner State.* Norman, Okla.: University of Oklahoma Press, 1964.

Mills, Robert K., Ed. *Implement & Tractor: Reflections on 100 Years of Farm Equipment.* Overland Park, Kansas: Intertec Publishing Co., 1986.

Minnes Album—Svenska Lutherska Församlingen, Salemsborg, Kansas, 1869-1909. Rock Island, Ill.: Augustana Book Concern, 1909.

Nystrom, Daniel B. *Scandinavian Christmas Traditions.* Apple Valley, Minn.: Twin Rainbow Press, 1987.

Russell, Don. *The Lives and Legends of Buffalo Bill.* Norman, Okla.: University of Oklahoma Press, 1960.

Seventy-Fifth Anniversary 1875-1950, Assaria Lutheran Church, Assaria, Kansas. Topeka, Kansas: Myers and Co., 1950.

Sichel, Marion. *The Victorians.* Boston: Plays, Inc.,1978.

St. Marie, Satenig and Flaherty, Carolyn. *Romantic Victorian Weddings, Then & Now.* New York: Dutton Studio Books, Penguin Group, 1991.

Tifft, Wilton S. *Ellis Island.* Chicago: Contemporary Books, Inc., 1990.

Todd, Verna Perrill. *Bridgeport Church and Community.* 1962.

U.S. Government records.

Vid Fyrtioårsfesten, Svenska Evangeliskt Lutherska Assaria Församlingen i Assaria, Kansas, Den 6-8 Okt. 1916.

NEWSPAPERS

The Assaria Argus

The Denver Post

The Lindsborg News

The Lindsborg Record

The McPherson Daily Republican

The Republican Journal

The Salina Sun

UNPUBLISHED MATERIAL

Assaria Lutheran Church records

Bethany College records

Bridgeport School records

Liberty Township records

Star School records

Wheeler School records

Also used were published and unpublished material listed in the bibliography of *Butter in the Well.*